On
Leading Digital Transformation

Sr. Beatrice Oguay
FSSA

HBR's 10 Must Reads series is the definitive collection of ideas and best practices for aspiring and experienced leaders alike. These books offer essential reading selected from the pages of *Harvard Business Review* on topics critical to the success of every manager.

Titles include:

On
Leading Digital
Transformation

HARVARD BUSINESS REVIEW PRESS
Boston, Massachusetts

HBR Press Quantity Sales Discounts

Harvard Business Review Press titles are available at significant quantity discounts when purchased in bulk for client gifts, sales promotions, and premiums. Special editions, including books with corporate logos, customized covers, and letters from the company or CEO printed in the front matter, as well as excerpts of existing books, can also be created in large quantities for special needs.

For details and discount information for both print and ebook formats, contact booksales@harvardbusiness.org, tel. 800-988-0886, or www.hbr.org/bulksales.

The web addresses referenced in this book were live and correct at the time of the book's publication but may be subject to change.

Library of Congress Cataloging-in-Publication data is forthcoming.

ISBN: 978-1-64782-216-3
eISBN: 978-1-64782-217-0

The paper used in this publication meets the requirements of the American National Standard for Permanence of Paper for Publications and Documents in Libraries and Archives Z39.48-1992.

Contents

Discovery-Driven Digital Transformation

by Rita McGrath and Ryan McManus

WHAT'S YOUR DIGITAL STRATEGY? That simple question often throws the CEOs of traditional companies into a panic. They believe that digital technologies and business models pose an existential threat to their way of doing business—and of course they're right. But the pressure they feel often leads them to make big bet-the-farm moves—and that's usually wrong.

Veon, a large multinational provider of telecommunications services, is a case in point. Its new digital platform, introduced in 2017, was a huge project, involving 100 staff members in Amsterdam and another hundred or so in its London office. The idea was to create a mobile app that would offer users rich localized experiences and serve as a sales channel for Veon's commercial partners (such as Mastercard). Management considered the project its top priority. But after being launched with much fanfare, the app got a lukewarm response from customers, and the effort to build a new ecosystem around it was scrapped. The failure led to a management exodus, layoffs, and a back-to-basics strategy with digital efforts sidelined to pilot-project stage.

Veon still needs a new business model, though, and clearly can't afford to make many more large investments in searching for one.

It doesn't have to. Just because a threat is huge doesn't mean that a response has to be. To the contrary, companies like Veon would actually be much better off taking a more incremental approach to

1

transformation over time. While they should always have a vision of where they want to go, they should work their way toward it by continually finding opportunities to digitize problematic processes in their core operations. When they tackle those projects, they'll learn what metrics to use, which assumptions to revise, where they can introduce new business models, and who their new competitors might be. And as they absorb those lessons, their understanding of their competitive landscape—and the long-term goals they set for themselves—will inevitably change.

There's already a process for this kind of ongoing learning approach to strategy: discovery-driven planning (DDP). One of us, Rita, and Ian MacMillan developed it in the 1990s as a product innovation methodology, and it was later incorporated into the popular "lean start-up" tool kit for launching businesses in an environment of high uncertainty. At its center is a low-cost process for quickly testing assumptions about what works, obtaining new information, and minimizing risks.

In the following pages we'll describe how an adapted form of DDP can help incumbent firms confront digital challenges and learn their way toward a new business model. Let's begin by looking in more detail at why a step-by-step transformation works better for traditional firms than the all-or-nothing approach that characterizes a start-up's pivot.

The Incremental Advantage of Incumbent Firms

Economists have long puzzled over why firms exist at all and, at a more granular level, which tasks belong within the boundaries of a given firm. One line of thought, begun by Ronald Coase in the 1930s, suggests that under certain conditions, market transactions often are not satisfactory for individuals: when it is difficult or expensive to get information about what you want to buy, when bargains are hard to strike because information is asymmetrical, and when it's costly or challenging to enforce agreements. If any of those conditions apply, it makes sense to keep the activities involved within a firm.

Idea in Brief

The Problem

Established companies spend billions trying to turn themselves into digitized orchestrators of some new ecosystem, only to fall flat on their faces.

Why It Happens

The CEOs believe that the existential threat posed by digital disrupters requires a gigantic, model-busting response.

The Solution

Adopt an incremental experimental approach: discovery-driven digital transformation. Look for problems to fix with digital technology, but exploit your rich knowledge of customers, broad operational scope, and deep talent pools while learning your way to a new business model.

Until fairly recently, the boundaries between firms and markets were well understood and relatively fixed. But digital technologies have changed all that by making it possible to use markets for a lot of work that once was done more efficiently within firms. Platforms such as Alibaba and Amazon have made it easy to outsource functions like selecting suppliers, negotiating prices, enforcing contracts, managing payments, and more.

As a result, executives in companies that were born digital have assumptions about how transactions should be structured that are completely different from those of executives in legacy companies. What's more, because digital firms' structures are evolving all the time, their managers revisit those assumptions frequently. Direct-to-consumer businesses (think Casper in mattresses, Harry's in shaving, and Warby Parker in eyeglasses) are constantly experimenting with and adjusting features like free shipping, product bundles, bonuses for adding items, and so on. Those tactics simply aren't available to an incumbent selling through distributors. And because the digital businesses cut out intermediaries, they can be profitable at a much lower scale.

A key consequence of all this is that digital start-ups can change direction, or pivot, without destroying much value. They usually aren't that capital-intensive and don't have big payrolls. The founders of Rooted, for instance, initially sold plants out of their apartment directly to consumers, only later moving to a separate space and hiring employees. For such companies, failure is relatively cheap—unless it happens late in the day (or investors succumb to the growth-at-all-costs mantra that is unraveling the fortunes of many so-called unicorns).

The employees, managers, and shareholders of traditional companies, however, cannot pivot without destroying value. If their digital gambles fail, workers lose their jobs, and physical assets have to be unloaded at fire-sale prices. And unlike the venture capitalists who back start-ups, the investors in what was once a safe company may not have the buffer of high-return investments to offset their losses.

But although incumbent firms can't pivot easily, the good news is that they don't need to. Think about what big companies can do that start-ups can't. Entrepreneurial ventures nearly always exploit a single idea. They usually can't try out multiple versions of the same idea at the same time, let alone multiple ideas. A big firm, in contrast, has the resources to explore a variety of ideas and can more easily experiment with different processes and operations, which makes it more likely to discover a dominant model than a start-up is. This also gives a large firm a better chance of responding effectively to a digital challenge.

Take the case of the German metals distributor Klöckner. Its CEO, Gisbert Rühl, wanted to build a digital platform for the entire industry—but he didn't sponsor a big-bang effort to create one. Instead, his goal was to build digital competencies gradually, while benefiting from the knowledge and insight of people working in the firm's core steel business. For the first two years Rühl focused on digitizing inefficient manual processes; the firm created an online shop, a contract portal, order transparency tools, and a parts-manager app. Through these efforts it learned enough to create a platform on which the company and customers could seamlessly interact.

Klöckner's story reveals another advantage that incumbent firms have, at least in the early stages of an industry's adoption of digital models. They're led by people who already know their customers and can mine rich databases of prior transactions for insights.

Start-ups are often led by technical experts and tend to be driven by new technical functionality rather than by the full portfolio of what customers are looking for. If you put a team of people who know the customers on the job, you'll stand a better chance of making your digital investment pay off. That's why Klöckner insisted that every project focus on how to help customers communicate more easily and efficiently with the company. That isn't the only goal to set, of course. Another company might start with a priority on shortening the time it takes to respond to a customer request. But whatever the goal is, it should frame the technology as an opportunity for the business rather than frame the business as an opportunity for the technology.

Once you accept the idea that firms should aim to disrupt in a nondisruptive manner, the challenge is subtly transformed from "What new business model should we back?" to the more nuanced question, "How can we learn our way toward a model that's right for our business?" That is where DDP comes in.

The Digital Context

DDP is somewhat like reverse engineering. When you use it in product development, you begin by imagining the offering you want to create and then figure out what you would need to change in order to get there. When you apply it to digital transformations, however, the focus is on reinventing the way you sell and deliver the products you already make as well as on identifying how to create and deliver new value through new digital capabilities.

Take power generation. Digital technologies are disrupting this once-stable industry, just as they are many other industries. Traditionally, power was generated from a central source and sent to its destination over a centrally managed grid. But new advances have made it possible to dynamically distribute power generated from dispersed small-scale producers tapping multiple energy sources. People with solar panels on their roofs or windmills in their gardens can sell surplus energy back to the grid, making households' cost of investing in power generation hardware more affordable and reducing the public's reliance on huge fossil-fuel power plants. If incumbents assume that the old business model will predict future success, they're likely to make big mistakes. General Electric's failed bet on the continued dominance of fossil-fuel-based electric plants provides a dramatic example.

Let's explore what's involved in applying a DDP approach to digital transformations. There are five key steps:

1. Define the operating experience: It's not just about digital
Before investing in a line of code, look for what isn't quite working in your operation. Where do you regularly need workarounds or have to stop a process unexpectedly to fetch more information or involve another person? These are likely to be areas that digitization can improve. Then think about how to redesign your operations there so that technology adds value, by making offerings and processes better, faster, cheaper, or more convenient.

The retailer Best Buy is one incumbent that was able to reconfigure its business operation in a way that created competitive advantages the digital-only players couldn't replicate. Back in 2010, Amazon released its price-comparison app, one of many tools that allowed shoppers to check out products in a physical store but order the same items at a discount online. Called "showrooming," the practice threatened to squeeze the lifeblood out of retail chains, which struggled to offer competitive prices while paying for real estate, staff, and inventory. It was one of the reasons Best Buy lost $1.7 billion in a single quarter in 2012.

Hubert Joly, the CEO hired to turn the company around, centered his strategy (and his business model) on solving two problems: negative comparable sales and declining operating margins. To do this, he envisioned a company that blended the human, the physical, and the digital in ways that an online-only player would find hard to match. He began by imagining what kind of customer experience Best Buy could deliver and, more important, identifying where it hadn't leveraged digital technologies to create that experience.

From this was born Best Buy's Renew Blue project, which had five components: a reinvigorated customer experience; a change in vendor partnerships; investments in ecological and social initiatives; the employee experience; and a return for investors. Financial targets and experiments were set up for each component.

To improve the employee experience, Best Buy launched initiatives focused on workforce morale, such as bringing back a popular employee discount that had been discontinued and investing in more-intensive training. To appeal to customers, the company began to match the prices of Amazon and other e-commerce players, which required a massive effort to overhaul Best Buy's warehousing, software, and supply chain activities. But because customers could walk out of the stores with the products, they could avoid the wait and the hassles (such as porch piracy) of having expensive products delivered, and that gave Best Buy an important edge. The company also created a system through which customers could order goods online for delivery or for pickup at the store. With 70% of Americans living within 15 miles of a Best Buy outlet, that approach proved to be extremely cost-effective.

Best Buy's new model turned the disadvantage of costly real estate into an advantage. At its more than 1,000 big-box locations, brands such as Apple, Samsung, and Microsoft created stores-within-stores, essentially paying rent to feature their offerings where real live shoppers could discover them in person. Best Buy is a neutral party to warring tech giants; archrivals Amazon and Google both sell their goods there. Finally, Best Buy invested in an in-home adviser capability, in which salaried, highly trained consultants go to customers' homes and provide tech help without selling anything. The goal is just to build stronger relationships with consumers. Throughout it all, Best Buy steadily transformed its digital footprint to support the strategy.

The Best Buy story illustrates the importance of being willing to rethink assumptions about how to use assets and engage with partners. Previous leaders in the firm had failed to see any way that it could price-match online retailers. But because Joly challenged traditional thinking, he spurred the company to reimagine relationships with vendors (which now pay to be in Best Buy stores) and redesign its supply chain so that the company's physical assets could support a new business model for competing with e-commerce giants.

2. Focus on specific problems: Identify outcomes and progress metrics

The key question in any digital-transformation strategy is, How can we use data and digital capabilities to create new value for our customers? The DDP process translates that challenge into clear project goals.

A traditional success metric for new projects, even today, is return on investment. But ROI doesn't help you understand what value a project adds for customers, at least not directly. Further, to calculate it you need to estimate both investments and returns, which is precisely what you haven't figured out yet. What you need to do instead is identify metrics that are more closely linked to the specific improvements you hope digital initiatives will bring about.

We typically collect all this information in a "from-to" table, which identifies a problem, describes what a solution would achieve, and proposes a way to measure progress on that solution. (For an example, see the exhibit "Tackling big change step-by-step.") As you work through solving these problems, you'll test and refine your assumptions—a key DDP discipline. You can also capture what you've spent to gain new insights and what they've saved you. Eventually, you can back into something similar to an ROI calculation.

At Klöckner, the ultimate goal was to change the business model in steel from marking up inventory to a services revenue model. At first, the digital initiatives were simple and were focused on improving the order process—by, for instance, replacing the faxing of orders with an online portal for ordering. With each one, performance on metrics such as turnaround time and the number of steps required to complete an order improved. As the company gained more knowledge and capabilities, its projects became more ambitious.

Of course, you still need a way to measure progress on digital transformation overall, and to do that we suggest a metric we call *return on time invested* (ROTI). To calculate it, you simply divide your total revenue by the number of employees. The idea is that successful technology investments should let you accomplish more with fewer people. For example, we used annual report data from 2018 to compare Amazon (a digital-first company) with Walmart

Tackling big change step-by-step

A key part of discovery-driven transformation is identifying organizational problems that can be addressed with digital technology, the desired improvement for each, and a metric for assessing progress toward it. All this information is captured in a tool called the from-to table. Below is how one financial services organization we've worked with filled its table out.

From	To	Progress metric
No consistent information about investments in a portfolio of projects; manual process	Clear and easily obtained information about investment flows; automated process	Reduction in time needed to update portfolio review information from 10 days to seconds
Significant effort needed to onboard new team members and bring them up to speed	Automated onboarding assistance that helps new team members learn the background of a project	Reduction in time it takes new team members to reach productivity from 30 days to five; high engagement scores among 85% of team members and top quadrant scores for psychological safety
No capture of learning created in one part of the organization for reuse elsewhere	Routine recording of project insights in a database that's searchable by keywords, geographies, and contexts	Information is shared by an average of 10 units in the organization; 50% decrease in duplicative experiments
Slow and inflexible financial and talent resource allocation across new opportunities	Dynamic prioritization and resource allocation driven by real-time data and discovery	Resource reallocation cycles go from quarterly or annually to weekly. Annual 50% to 100% increase in number of experiments with strategic options

(a more-traditional legacy business). We found that Amazon had $232.9 billion in net sales and 647,500 full- and part-time workers. Its sales per employee were $359,671. In contrast, Walmart had $495.8 billion in net sales and 2.3 million associates. Its sales per employee were $215,548. Amazon enjoyed 67% higher performance per employee.

3. Identify your competition: Cast a wide net

Industry boundaries have blurred so much that standard industrial classification (SIC) codes are more or less useless. This by itself is one reason why conventional strategy-making approaches predicated on boundary assumptions are failing incumbents.

We suggest that leaders instead think about the field of competition not as a marketplace where similar players offer rival products and services but as what strategists call an arena. An arena is defined by a customer need—what Clay Christensen dubbed the "job to be done." It's a notion that goes back to Ted Levitt, who recommended that railway companies see themselves as competing in the transportation business against airlines, buses, trucking, and even cars. If railway passengers are a market, transportation users constitute an arena.

Smart born-digital firms already think this way. For example, Netflix has been very clear that it doesn't intend to compete just against television or the movies for viewers' time. It intends to compete against every possible leisure activity that a person might do instead of watching streaming content. The company sees traditional media companies as its rivals, of course, but its leadership looks at magazines, books, podcasts, and sporting events as competition as well.

At this point in the process, you should go back and determine whether the outcomes and metrics of success you spelled out in steps one and two are reasonable, given the arena you're competing in. Is your category losing share of wallet to others in the arena, for instance, or holding its own? Netflix has plenty of room to meet its growth goals, because total hours of video viewing are increasing and a lot of that growth is from streaming video.

4. Look for platforms: Don't forget the ecosystem implications
In the digital economy, striving to become an intermediary through which others buy and sell goods is an extremely popular strategy. It's a tempting business model, because once the two sides of a market have joined a platform they have little incentive to jump to another. This is partly due to network effects, whereby a platform's value to any user increases as the number of other users on that platform rises. Airbnb, for instance, benefits when more hosts and more guests use it and has historically gone to great lengths to ensure the loyalty of both.

A platform is also attractive because it needs less capital. To run a conventional hotel, you have to have real estate, rooms that need to be looked after, reservation systems, staff, and so on. Airbnb, in contrast, taps an ecosystem of hosts to provide all those things, and its directly controlled activities are simply to match hosts and guests and guarantee transactions, both of which occur entirely in the cloud and thus are infinitely scalable.

To understand whether a platform opportunity exists, we use a tool we call a *customer consumption chain* (introduced in HBR in 1997). The idea is simple: that as customers try to get jobs done in their lives, they go through a series of experiences, beginning with awareness of a need, then working through how to get that need met, and going all the way to the conclusion of a service or the end of a product's life. Digital technologies make open-market transactions for many links in that chain possible, allowing firms to build platforms.

That sounds like bad news for established organizations. But they have an ace in the hole: They employ many people who have deep technical expertise or understand customer problems. Those capabilities can give them an edge in identifying platformlike opportunities and building ecosystems. At Klöckner, Rühl realized that once there was price transparency—and far less friction—in the trading of basic metal commodities, competitive advantage would shift to suppliers that could offer superior solutions and service. The company blended the new ways of operating on platforms (co-creating designs with customers, for instance) of its digital arm with its workforce's deep expertise (in, say, manufacturing with 3-D lasers) to develop customized, higher-value offerings.

Becoming a popular platform isn't easy for corporations. The business landscape is littered with would-be platforms that failed even though they seemed to have all the right components. General Electric's Predix initiative, which was intended to be the platform for the industrial internet of things, is an example. Rather than driving the digitization of services that customers would value, Predix was sucked into serving primarily internal GE units—and a lot of them. Further, as part of GE Digital, the initiative was given P&L responsibility, which oriented it toward short-term contracts with customers that could pay some bills in the interim. It also took on way too much too soon, rather than proceeding by finding a good fit for its capabilities and building from there.

5. Test your assumptions: Failures are lessons too

One of the more popular tools to come out of DDP is the assumption checkpoint table. To create one, just write down the next few milestones that your digital project will go through, which assumptions need to be tested at each, and if possible, how much that test will cost. The beauty of this approach is that it moves the conversation from "Oh, you were wrong, that was a failure" to "Was it worth that price to learn what we needed to learn?"

Consider how Buffer, a service that allows people to space out social media promotions without having to predetermine the timing, tested assumptions in its launch phase. Joel Gascoigne, Buffer's cofounder, got the idea for the business from his own frustration with how clunky it was to try to tweet more consistently.

The first assumption he wanted to test was whether anybody else perceived this to be a problem. So he built a very simple two-page website. The first page's pitch was "Tweet More Consistently with Buffer." If users clicked on it, they were taken to a second page, with the heading "Hello, You Caught Us Before We're Ready," which had a place for people to enter their email addresses if they were interested in Buffer's solution. Most people weren't, but some were. So Gascoigne added a third page between the other two to test pricing hypotheses. And again, most people weren't interested in paying, but enough were to persuade Gascoigne to build the product.

Next he had to decide how complex to make it and how many social platforms to apply it to. He ended up keeping it very simple and supporting only Twitter at first. As of 2018, Buffer had more than 1.4 million social accounts connected to its apps.

Many large corporations have adopted a similar test-and-learn mindset. Several new services make experimentation easier—for example, Alpha, whose subscribers use it to obtain fast feedback about products from potential customers before making expensive or irreversible decisions. At WellMatch, an Aetna business unit, experimentation helped resolve disagreements about design decisions. According to Etugo Nwokah, the former chief product officer, one area of disagreement involved its website: Every group in the unit wanted to have its content appear on the landing page. The trial entry page ended up being so busy that it confused consumers. The company had to go back to the drawing board and do a redesign—but was able to do so at a much lower cost and risk than if the webpage had been launched for real.

The Payoff

Digital transformation is complex and requires new ways of approaching strategy. Starting big, spending a lot, and assuming you have all the information is likely to produce a full-on attack from corporate antibodies—everything from risk aversion and resentment of your project to simple resistance to change.

A discovery-driven approach gets leaders past the common barriers to digital transformation. By starting small, spending a little on an ongoing portfolio of experiments, and learning a lot, you can win early supporters and early adopters. By then moving quickly and demonstrating clear impact on financial performance indicators, you can build a case for and learn your way into a digital strategy. You can also use your digitization projects to begin an organizational transformation. As people become more comfortable with the horizontal communications and activities that digital technologies enable, they will also embrace new ways of working.

Incumbent companies have some great advantages over new competitors: paying customers, financial resources, customer and market data, and larger talent pools. But CEOs will have to integrate agility and innovation into their broader organizations and communicate the new ways of digital thinking while minimizing disruption to their existing businesses. A discovery-driven approach provides a way to address those challenges.

Originally published in May–June 2020. Reprint R2003J

The Transformative Business Model

by Stelios Kavadias, Kostas Ladas, and Christoph Loch

WE USUALLY ASSOCIATE an industry's transformation with the adoption of a new technology. But although new technologies are often major factors, they have never transformed an industry on their own. What does achieve such a transformation is a business model that can link a new technology to an emerging market need.

MP3 technology is a classic case in point. Early MP3 devices represented an order-of-magnitude increase in capacity over magnetic tapes and CDs: Users could carry thousands of songs on a small device. But MP3 players revolutionized the audio devices market only after Apple coupled the iPod with iTunes in a new business model, swiftly moving music-recording sales from the physical to the virtual world.

What, exactly, enables a business model to deliver on a technology's potential? To answer that question, we embarked on an in-depth analysis of 40 companies that had launched new business models in a variety of industries. Some succeeded in radically altering their industries; others looked promising but ultimately did not succeed. In this article we present the key takeaways from our research and suggest how they can help innovators transform industries.

How Business Models Work

Definitions of "business model" vary, but most people would agree that it describes how a company creates and captures value. The features of the model define the customer value proposition and the pricing mechanism, indicate how the company will organize itself and whom it will partner with to produce value, and specify how it will structure its supply chain. Basically, a business model is a system whose various features interact, often in complex ways, to determine the company's success.

In any given industry, a dominant business model tends to emerge over time. In the absence of market distortions, the model will reflect the most efficient way to allocate and organize resources. Most attempts to introduce a new model fail—but occasionally one succeeds in overturning the dominant model, usually by leveraging a new technology. If new entrants use the model to displace incumbents, or if competitors adopt it, then the industry has been transformed.

Consider Airbnb, which upended the hotel industry. Founded in 2008, the company has experienced phenomenal growth: It now has more rooms than either InterContinental Hotels or Hilton Worldwide. As of this writing, Airbnb represents 19.5% of the hotel room supply in New York and operates in 192 countries, in which it accounts for 5.4% of room supply (up from 3.6% in 2015).

The founders of Airbnb realized that platform technology made it feasible to craft an entirely new business model that would challenge the traditional economics of the hotel business. Unlike conventional hotel chains, Airbnb does not own or manage property—it allows users to rent any livable space (from a sofa to a mansion) through an online platform that matches individuals looking for accommodations with home owners willing to share a room or a house. Airbnb manages the platform and takes a percentage of the rent.

Because its income does not depend on owning or managing physical assets, Airbnb needs no large investments to scale up and thus can charge lower prices (usually 30% lower than hotels charge). Moreover, since the home owners are responsible for managing and maintaining the property and any services they may offer, Airbnb's risks (not to mention operational costs) are much lower than those of traditional hotels. On the customer side, Airbnb's model redefines the value proposition by offering a more personal service—and a cheaper one.

Before platform technology existed, there was no reason to change the hotel business in any meaningful way. But after its

Idea in Brief

The Question

No new technology can transform an industry unless a business model can link it to an emerging market need. How can you tell whether a model will succeed in doing that?

The Research

The authors undertook an in-depth analysis of 40 companies that launched new business models in a variety of industries. Some had transformed their industries; others looked promising but ultimately didn't succeed.

The Findings

Transformative business models tend to include three or more of these features: (1) personalization, (2) a closed-loop process, (3) asset sharing, (4) usage-based pricing, (5) a collaborative ecosystem, and (6) an agile and adaptive organization.

introduction, the dominant business model became vulnerable to attack from anyone who could leverage that technology to create a more compelling value proposition for customers. The new business model serves as the interface between *what technology enables* and *what the marketplace wants*.

Let's look now at what features make a business model transformative.

The Six Keys to Success

We selected the 40 new business models we analyzed on the basis of how many mentions they received in the high-quality, high-circulation business press. All of them seemed to have the *potential* to transform their industries, but only a subset had succeeded in doing so. We looked for recurring features in the models and found six. No company displayed all of them, but as we shall see, a higher number of these features usually correlated with a higher chance of success at transformation.

1. **A more personalized product or service.** Many new models offer products or services that are better tailored than the dominant models to customers' individual and immediate needs. Companies often leverage technology to achieve this at competitive prices.

2. **A closed-loop process.** Many models replace a linear consumption process (in which products are made, used, and then disposed of) with a closed loop, in which used products are recycled. This shift reduces overall resource costs.

3. **Asset sharing.** Some innovations succeed because they enable the sharing of costly assets—Airbnb allows home owners to share them with travelers, and Uber shares assets with car owners. Sometimes assets may be shared across a supply chain. The sharing typically happens by means of two-sided online marketplaces that unlock value for both sides: I get money from renting my spare room, and you get a cheaper and perhaps nicer place to stay. Sharing also reduces entry barriers to many industries, because an entrant need not own the assets in question; it can merely act as an intermediary.

4. **Usage-based pricing.** Some models charge customers when they use the product or service, rather than requiring them to buy something outright. The customers benefit because they incur costs only as offerings generate value; the company benefits because the number of customers is likely to grow.

5. **A more collaborative ecosystem.** Some innovations are successful because a new technology improves collaboration with supply chain partners and helps allocate business risks more appropriately, making cost reductions possible.

6. **An agile and adaptive organization.** Innovators sometimes use technology to move away from traditional hierarchical models of decision making in order to make decisions that better reflect market needs and allow real-time adaptation to changes in those needs. The result is often greater value for the customer at less cost to the company.

Each feature on this list is tied to long-term trends in both technology and demand. (See the exhibit "Linking technology and the market.") On the tech side, one trend is the development of sensors that allow cheaper and broader data capture. Another is that big data, artificial intelligence, and machine learning are enabling

Linking technology and the market

The six features that characterize successful innovation all link a recognized technology trend and a recognized market need. Trends were identified by an analysis of regularly published industry reports from think tanks and consulting companies such as the McKinsey Global Institute, PwC, and the Economist Intelligence Unit.

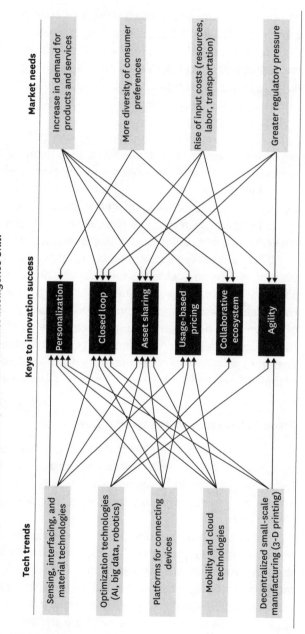

Tech trends

Sensing, interfacing, and material technologies

Optimization technologies (AI, big data, robotics)

Platforms for connecting devices

Mobility and cloud technologies

Decentralized small-scale manufacturing (3-D printing)

Keys to innovation success

Personalization

Closed loop

Asset sharing

Usage-based pricing

Collaborative ecosystem

Agility

Market needs

Increase in demand for products and services

More diversity of consumer preferences

Rise of input costs (resources, labor, transportation)

Greater regulatory pressure

companies to turn enormous amounts of unstructured data into rules and decisions. A third is that connected devices (the internet of things) and cloud technology are permitting decentralized and widespread data manipulation and analysis. And a fourth is that developments in manufacturing (think nanotechnology and 3-D printing) are creating more possibilities for distributed and small-scale production.

On the market side, although the steady progress of developing countries has led to a stable increase in demand worldwide, it is complicated by a greater diversity in customer preferences (both across and within countries). Higher factor prices (despite the commodity price reductions of 2015) and heightened regulation (notably on environmental effects and business conduct) further increase the challenges for companies looking to gain market share.

All six features represent potential solutions for linking market demand and technological capability. For example, greater personalization in the value proposition responds to the fragmentation of consumer preferences and the resultant demand for more-diverse offerings. That personalization has been made possible by sensors that collect data from connected devices via the cloud; the data is analyzed by big data solutions and turned into services—such as recommendations and alerts—that are different for each user.

From Innovation to Transformation

In theory, the more of the six features a new business model has, the greater its potential to transform a given industry should be. We tested that hypothesis by analyzing how many features each of the 40 new models displayed and comparing the results with its actual performance.

We gave each model one point for each feature on which it outperformed the incumbent business model. We then assessed its transformative success according to the degree to which the model had attracted market share (displacing incumbents) and the extent to which other companies had copied it. Our results strongly suggest (that's the best one can get from statistical analyses) that business models with transformative potential tend to have three or more of the six features. (See the exhibit "How many boxes should a model tick?")

The taxi service company Uber ticks no fewer than five boxes. Its business model is built on asset sharing—the drivers use their own cars. Uber has developed a *collaborative ecosystem* in which the driver assumes the risk of winning rides, while the platform helps minimize that risk through the application of big data. The platform also creates *agility* through an internal decision-making system that responds to market changes in real time. This lets Uber apply *usage-based pricing* and direct drivers to locations where the probability of finding a fare is high.

Finally, Uber uses a scheme whereby customers rate drivers. Via the big data platform, a would-be customer can see on his or her mobile device the closest drivers and their ratings. The rating system pushes drivers to offer clean cars and quality service, and it also provides at least a bit of *personalization*. Allowing the customer to decide between the closest car and the one (maybe a bit farther out) with the highest rating may not sound like much, but it is still far ahead of traditional taxi services.

The implication of our finding is straightforward: If you are thinking about changing your business model or entering an industry with a new model, you can rate yourself on how well your model performs on the six features. If you don't beat the competition on any of them, your chances of success are low. But if your model significantly outdoes the current model on three or more features, you are well positioned to succeed.

To rate yourself on a feature, you must first define what it actually means in your industry. For example, in financial services *personalization* may mean tailored loan terms (including interest rates, monthly payments, and loan duration), whereas in retail it may mean customized T-shirt designs or one-off dresses. In education it may mean that the support provided to students changes according to their individual strengths and weaknesses, and in health care it may mean data-enabled, targeted medicine. Only when performance is expressed in such industry-specific ways can a company develop

How many boxes should a model tick?

Our research suggests that to transform an industry, a business model must display at least three of the six key features.
Here's how the 40 new models we examined stacked up.

	Business	Industry	Personalization	Closed loop	Asset sharing	Usage-based pricing	Collaborative ecosystem	Agility	Score
1	Airbnb	Real estate	X		X		X	X	4
2	Alibaba	Retail	X			X	X		3
3	Amazon	Retail	X			X	X	X	4
4	Appear Here	Real estate rentals			X		X		2
5	Apple iPod	Electronics	X			X	X		3
6	Arm	Electronics	X				X	X	3
7	Canon	Electronics/copiers		X		X	X		3
8	Coursera	Education	X				X	X	2
9	Dell	Electronics	X			X	X	X	4
10	EdX	Education	X				X		2
11	Etsy	Retail	X						1
12	Google AdWords	Advertising	X			X	X	X	4
13	Handy	Home services				X	X		2

	Business	Industry	Personalization	Closed loop	Asset sharing	Usage-based pricing	Collaborative ecosystem	Agility	Score
14	IKEA	Retail	X	X			X	X	4
15	Interface	Carpeting		X		X			2
16	JustPark	Real estate	X		X	X			3
17	LEGO Factory	Toys	X			X	X	X	4
18	Lending Club	Banking				X	X	X	2
19	LiveOps	Call centers			X			X	3
20	Lyft	Taxi operation	X		X	X	X		4
21	M-Pesa	Banking	X		X		X		3
22	Medicast	Health care	X		X		X		3
23	Natura	Cosmetics		X			X		2
24	Nike ID	Footwear	X					X	2
25	Philips pay per lux	Lighting		X	X	X	X		4
26	Ricoh pay per page	Electronics		X		X	X		3
27	Rolls-Royce power-by-the-hour	Engines		X		X	X	X	4
28	Ryanair	Transportation				X	X	X	3
29	Salesforce.com	Software	X		X	X			3

(continued)

How many boxes should a model tick? (Continued)

	Business	Industry	Personalization	Closed loop	Asset sharing	Usage-based pricing	Collaborative ecosystem	Agility	Score
30	Shyp	Transport & logistics	X	X			X		3
31	TaskRabbit	Home services			X	X			2
32	Tencent QQ	Software	X			X	X		3
33	Uber	Taxi operation	X		X	X	X	X	5
34	Udacity	Education	X				X		2
35	Washio	Dry cleaning	X		X	X			3
36	Wayfair	Home goods		X			X	X	3
37	Xerox	Electronics				X		X	2
38	Zara	Apparel	X				X	X	3
39	Zipcar	Transportation	X		X	X		X	4
40	Zopa	Banking	X		X	X		X	4

metrics to evaluate and compare its model on the key features and begin to think about how to differentiate itself by using new technologies.

Healx: A Case Study

Informed by our business model framework, we advised (and Cambridge Judge Business School's business accelerator supported) the tech venture Healx, which focuses on the treatment of patients with rare diseases in the emerging field of personalized medicine. A big challenge for pharmaceutical companies in this domain is that rare-disease markets are very small, so companies usually have to charge astronomical prices. (One drug, Soliris, used in the treatment of paroxysmal nocturnal hemoglobinuria, costs about $500,000 per patient-year.) Some potential treatments are, however, being used for more-common diseases with large patient markets. They could be repurposed to suit the needs of rare-disease sufferers, but they typically work only for people with specific genetic profiles.

Enter Healx, with a platform that leverages big data technology and analytics across multiple databases owned by various organizations within global life sciences and health care to efficiently match treatments to rare-disease patients. Its initial business model hit three of our six key features. First, Healx's value proposition was about *asset sharing* (for example, making available clinical-trial databases that record the effectiveness of most drugs across therapeutic areas and diseases, including rare ones). Second, the business promised more *personalization* by revealing drugs with high potential for treating the rare diseases covered. Finally, Healx's model would, in theory, create a *collaborative ecosystem* by bringing together big pharma (which has the treatment and trial data) and health care providers (which have data about effectiveness and incompatibility reactions and also personal genome descriptions).

How did we measure performance along those features? To assess *personalization,* we compared the amount of drug data currently provided to sufferers of rare diseases with the amount that Healx could provide, which initially covered 1,000 of the 7,000 rare diseases that have formal advocacy groups worldwide. These groups represent some 350 million people, 95% of whom currently get no even reasonably relevant drug recommendations. We measured *asset sharing* by looking at the proportion of known data on rare-disease-relevant drugs that Healx could access—about 20% in its start-up phase. Finally, we assessed its *collaborative ecosystem* by looking at how many of the main data-holding institutions participated—about a quarter.

At first Healx struggled to get pharma companies to join the platform; they were concerned that their treatment data would leak to competitors. But the Healx team spotted an opportunity to give companies an incentive. In 2014 the United Kingdom's National Health Service introduced a new rule for pharmaceutical companies: If an expensive treatment doesn't work for a patient, the company responsible can be forced to reimburse NHS providers for its cost. The reimbursement amounts were disease-specific and counted in the thousands of British pounds.

Treatment failure is often caused by specificities in individual genomes, and Healx's managers realized that their technology could help companies predict such failures with high accuracy, potentially saving millions of pounds a year.

More recently, Healx has developed a machine-learning algorithm that can use a patient's biological information not only to match drugs to disease symptoms but also to predict exactly which drug will achieve what level of effectiveness for that particular patient. The latest version of its business model brings *personalization* to the maximum possible level and adds *agility,* because the treating clinician—armed with the biological data and the algorithm—can make better treatment decisions directly with the patient and doesn't have to rely on fixed rules of thumb about which of the few available off-label drugs to use. In this way, Healx is able to support decentralized, real-time, accurate decision making.

This version of the Healx model has even more transformation potential—it exhibits four of the six features; it has already generated revenue from customers; and in the long term it could empower patients by giving them much more information before they consult a medical practitioner. Although it is still too early to tell whether that potential will be realized, Healx is clearly a venture to watch. It has earned a number of prizes (including the 2015 Life Science Business of the Year and the 2016 Graduate Business of the Year in the Cambridge cluster) and sizable investments from several global funds.

You cannot guarantee the success of an innovation (unless you choose a market niche so small as to be insignificant). But you can load the dice by ensuring that your business model links market needs with emerging technologies. The more such links you can make, the more likely you are to transform your industry.

Originally published in October 2016. Reprint R1610H

Digital Doesn't Have to Be Disruptive

by Nathan Furr and Andrew Shipilov

NEAR THE END OF A LONG LUNCH overlooking tranquil Lake Geneva, a senior vice president at a leading global company confessed to us: "We have a dozen committees on digital transformation; we have digital transformation initiatives; we are going full steam on digital transformation . . . but no one can explain to me what it actually means."

At a very basic level, the answer is simple: The much-used term simply means adapting an organization's strategy and structure to capture opportunities enabled by digital technology. This is not a new challenge—after all, computers and software have been around for decades and have brought changes both to products and services and to how we make and deliver them. But the point the SVP was making is that it has become increasingly difficult for a company to translate that answer into an action plan. Computers today can fit in your pocket or on your wrist, and the software applications that run on them increasingly enable the automation of tasks traditionally done by humans (such as managing expenses), the virtualization of hardware, and ever more targeted product and service customization. What's more, these apps can reach people everywhere: Sensors embedded in devices and interfaces permit the real-time feed of data, allowing even more informed decision making and machine-driven recommendations. In short, digital technology is no longer in the cordoned-off domain of IT; it is being applied to almost every part of a company's value chain. Thus it's entirely understandable that managers struggle to grasp what digital transformation actually means for them in terms of which opportunities to pursue and which initiatives to prioritize.

Faced with this reality, it's not surprising that many managers expect digital transformation to involve a radical disruption of the business, huge new investments in technology, a complete switch from physical to virtual channels, and the acquisition of tech start-ups. To be sure, in some cases such a paradigm shift *is* involved. But our research and work suggest that for most companies, digital transformation means something very different from outright disruption, in which the old is swept away by the new. Change is involved, and sometimes radical replacements for manufacturing processes, distribution channels, or business models are necessary; but more often than not, transformation means incremental steps to better deliver the core value proposition.

In the following pages we draw on the insights we have gathered—from interviews with more than 60 companies and from the hundreds of senior leaders with whom we have interacted while teaching—to dispel some critical myths about digital transformation and to offer executives a better understanding of how businesses need to respond to the current trends.

Myth: Digital requires radical disruption of the value proposition

Reality: It usually means using digital tools to better serve the known customer need

Some managers believe that to achieve a digital transformation, they must dramatically alter their company's value proposition or risk suffering a tidal wave of disruption. As a result, at the start of many digital transformations, companies aspire to be like Apple and try to find a new high-tech core product or platform that will serve brand-new customer needs. Although some might succeed, we believe that the customer needs most companies serve will look much the same as before. The challenge is to find the best way to serve those

Idea in Brief

The Problem

Many managers believe that digital transformation involves a radical disruption of the business, new investments in technology, a complete switch from physical to virtual channels, and the acquisition of tech start-ups.

Why It Happens

Digital technology is being applied to almost every part of

company value chains, making it difficult for managers to identify priorities.

How to Fix It

The authors dispel five critical myths about digital transformation and offer executives a better understanding of how to respond to current trends.

needs using digital tools. As the senior executive of Galeries Lafayette, a high-end French fashion retailer, told us, "This is another modernization. We have been around for more than 100 years, and we have had to undergo other changes in our history, such as the arrival of hypermarkets, shopping malls, specialty chains, fast fashion, brands becoming retailers, and finally e-commerce."

The shipping container company Maersk provides a good example of what this executive meant. The costs of shipping are affected by global trade barriers and inefficiency in international supply chains. The industry also suffers from a lack of transparency. These are familiar challenges. What digital did for Maersk was provide a new way of overcoming them. The company partnered with IBM and government authorities to deploy blockchain technology for fast and secure access to end-to-end supply chain information from a single source. The technology, coupled with an ability to receive real-time sensor data, allows trustworthy cross-organization workflows, lower administrative expenses, and better risk assessments in global shipments. This shift allows Maersk to serve its core customers better. But Maersk has not been transformed into Google. It remains a company whose value proposition is providing a fast, reliable, cost-efficient shipping service—one with the potential to be more streamlined and transparent, thanks to a smart leveraging of digital technology.

Another good example is the Russian airline Aeroflot, which has transformed itself from one of the world's worst airlines into one of the best, with a Net Promoter Score that rose from 44% in 2010 to 72% in 2016 and a passenger load that grew from 64.5% in 2009 to 81.3% in 2016, according to company data. How? The airline used digital technology to significantly improve core activities: operations, reporting, passenger booking, scheduling, and customer care. Specifically, it created dashboards that provide management with an instant overview of more than 450 key performance indicators. The company also aggregates information from sensors installed on the planes, allowing visibility into aircraft performance and preventive maintenance and thereby reducing operating costs. The PR department was even able to lower its headcount, because responding to journalists' inquiries about company data now requires less effort: It's all available on the dashboard. In addition, Aeroflot repurposed the digital architecture created to run the main airline to simultaneously run a low-cost carrier—something few other airlines have succeeded in doing. Once again, nothing has altered the company's raison d'être: It remains a passenger airline, selling seats on planes to many different destinations. It's just a more efficient and user-friendly one through the use of digital tools.

This is not to say that disruption doesn't occur. Make no mistake: Things are changing quickly, and companies that do nothing will be either disrupted or at a minimum outcompeted by those that transform using digital tools. But even in the classic industries where disruption strikes hardest, the story is always a little more complicated when you look below the surface. Whether you are disrupted or not always depends on the job you do for customers. If an incumbent can use digital tools to meet customers' needs better than a disruptive new entrant can, it will still prosper.

Take the taxi business. Uber's impact on taxis is one of the most frequently cited examples of digital disruption. The public remembers taxi drivers' striking around the world—notably including in Paris, our hometown—in the face of what seemed to be an existential threat to their livelihoods. But today taxi companies in Paris are thriving.

G7 is a traditional taxi company founded in 1905. It once had a reputation in Paris, as did many other taxi companies, for its drivers' rudeness. Fast-forward to the present: Like Uber, G7 has developed an app that allows customers to book a taxi. The app offers various service levels: sharing, regular cab, green (hybrid or electric), van, and VIP. You can use the app to hail a car from the curb, or you can jump into one standing at the corner, and you can pay the driver with the app using his or her four-digit code.

But G7 differs from Uber in some important ways: Its drivers are better trained, the cars are cleaner, and you can prebook a ride for exactly the time you want it, instead of in a 15-minute window. More important, although a G7 might be slightly more expensive on average than an Uber, it is vastly less expensive when you most need it: Uber imposes surge pricing, multiplying your fare twofold, threefold, or even eightfold, while G7's prices remain constant. It's clear that Uber's arrival forced traditional taxi companies to improve their service: G7 drivers now take etiquette lessons. But it's hard to argue that the advent of digital necessitated a wholesale reinvention of G7's value proposition.

Likewise, the hotel business has been among the industries most threatened by the rise of digital technologies, first from OTA (over-the-air) players like Expedia, next from platforms like Airbnb, and now from search providers like Google. When we interviewed Marriott's CEO, Arne Sorenson, about the impact of digital technologies, he didn't downplay the threat. "The digital forces are clearly very revolutionary and powerful and can be frightening at times," he said. "We are in an absolute war for who owns the customer."

Sorenson emphasized that technology would be a major factor in winning the war: "We have to make sure we are using technology to be more efficient in our operations, deliver service, and create a great loyalty digital platform, but also make sure we have a platform that is big enough and delivers value to our customers so that they book directly with us. We are not going to out-Google Google, but we want to make sure we have a community of folks who can relate to us. It must be through a digital platform. But that platform is about engaging our customers." And that is something Marriott has always done. Although it has launched platforms to compete with Airbnb and drive customers directly to its own site, it's also focusing on what it does best—delivering a great hotel and customer experience. Those who have stayed with Marriott or its sister company Starwood know they're unlikely to get the luxurious mattress and bedding these hotels are famous for at a typical Airbnb.

Understanding that digital transformation does not change the reason your business exists will help you identify the technologies you should focus on. Managers who believe that digital disruption requires wholesale reinvention of the core business end up running in a thousand directions. But if the challenge is simply to better address their customers' jobs to be done, they will most likely focus on the technologies that have the greatest effect on their customers (such as customer experience or relationship synergies) or their core capabilities (such as cost synergies). Your company, just like Maersk, Aeroflot, and G7, can probably continue to serve the same core customers even in the digital era. And the needs of those customers won't change—although digital will certainly provide a better way of catering to them.

Myth: Digital will replace physical

Reality: It's a "both/and"

There is no doubt that digital often enables the elimination of inefficient intermediaries and costly physical infrastructure. But that doesn't mean the physical goes away entirely. In fact, as has been well documented, many retailers are finding ways to create a hybrid of physical and digital that taps into the advantages of each. And it's not just retailers—the same trend can be seen in many other consumer-facing businesses.

In retail, Galeries Lafayette provides a classic example. Despite intense competition from online stores, GL recognizes the importance of physical proximity to the customer, which only a brick-and-mortar store can offer. Both models have advantages: Physical helps build an emotional relationship with customers, while digital (especially AI) helps better understand customers' needs. Whereas in the past companies focused too much on the product and not enough on the customer, hybrid models can put the customer at the center of the business.

To ensure that it builds both an understanding of and an emotional connection with customers, the company is seamlessly blending the physical and digital worlds in its new store on the Champs-Élysées. The store will carry a curated selection of luxury items, and it will be staffed by salespeople hired for their ability to interact with visitors to the store, their expertise in fashion and style, and their facility with social media. These staffers, known as personal shoppers or personal stylists, will establish emotional relationships with their customers, making the physical store an initial customer attraction and touch point. Shoppers can then embark on digitally enabled transactions. The new technology will also help salespeople "remember" customers and their preferences and identify individualized perks that will appeal to them.

GL has already gone partway down this road at its flagship Boulevard Haussmann store, where employees are equipped with tablets. Customers come to the store having obtained—through online searches—a lot more information about some products than the salespeople have. The tablets allow employees to quickly browse the online catalogue and become equally well informed.

Shoppers value a physical store visit because they can see and feel actual products. They can reserve items online and try them out in the store without obligation. Alternatively, they can buy products online and simply pick them up in the store. In either case, salespeople must understand how to act like personal shoppers, and the product and customer data they have enable them to do so.

Many digital-first brands are converging on the same path. Bonobos, for example, which was born pure digital, now uses physical stores to let customers try on clothes. After a purchase the clothes are mailed directly from a centrally managed inventory. Warby Parker, another digital native, also now uses physical stores to create welcoming customer experiences. Like GL, these retailers are serving needs that digital meets poorly—creating emotional connections and dealing with the challenges of fitting clothing or eyewear—while using technology to leverage data and achieve cost efficiencies.

We're seeing something similar in the energy sector. Several electric utility companies in Europe have effectively combined the advantages of physical and digital in their connected home systems, which contain smart thermostats and a variety of sensors and detectors. Google and Amazon have entered the market for smart home devices, but utilities have the advantage of engineers (or selected contractors) who back the smart thermostats' value proposition—and customers trust those people to do installation, maintenance, and repair. Some of these companies enable preventive maintenance: If a sensor indicates that a heating system is about to break, the customer is alerted through the thermostat and can schedule an engineer's visit in advance. The same alert helps the engineer understand the problem before the visit and arrive with the right equipment to fix it. This seamless integration of physical and digital can significantly reduce visits and parts used while granting the customer peace of mind.

TUI UK, a travel agency, has also turned to a hybrid of physical and digital. Initially it occupied a very precarious place—its industry is broadly viewed as being disrupted. But as it embarked on a digital transformation, the company discovered that although many customers wanted to make their travel plans digitally, they also wanted to interact with people in retail locations, asking questions and becoming comfortable with complex itineraries.

Myth: Digital involves buying start-ups

Reality: It involves protecting start-ups

Often companies try to access new technologies or ideas by acquiring start-ups and then integrating them. This approach risks killing the start-up's culture and chasing away the talent acquired during its creation. Smart companies prefer to build hybrid relationships with start-ups—strong enough to learn and find synergies but weak enough to avoid destroying the culture. So even though they may own the start-ups, they allow them to operate as semi-independent businesses.

Avnet, a $19 billion global technology solutions provider, is a good example. The company made two important digital acquisitions: Hackster.io, a platform that allows makers from around the world to post their ideas for new products (such as sensors to monitor city noise and pollution levels, augmented reality headsets, and baby oxygen monitors), and Dragon Innovation, a start-up that helps companies bridge the gap between made-for-prototype and industrial-scale electronic products. These companies operate as semi-independent entities and interact with Avnet through Dayna Badhorn, its vice president for emerging businesses. Her role is to protect the acquired companies from the inefficiencies—such as excessive planning and slow product development cycles—of the parent organization while helping Avnet learn agility and the importance of doing quick experiments. Hackster and Dragon Innovation call her their guardian angel.

The importance of a guardian angel is underlined by Galeries Lafayette's experience with its start-up accelerator, Lafayette Plug and Play, in which several big traditional retailers, including Richemont, Carrefour, Lagardère Travel, and Kiabi, are partners. Although GL executives spend a lot of time interacting with start-ups in the accelerator, the company struggled at first to translate such interactions into tangible projects inside GL, because no project leader was assigned to follow through. The situation has improved since GL appointed a manager to fill that role. GL does not buy start-ups from the accelerator (to avoid killing their innovative culture), so having someone to permanently liaise with them helps it maintain close relationships with accelerator members and implement the resulting initiatives. The other corporate members have followed suit, and their uptake of collaborations has improved as well.

In each case a guardian angel fights to take advantage of the best of both organizations, not only helping the start-up hold fast to its mission (which is what motivates much of the talent to stay) but also linking it to the mission of the larger organization while protecting the start-up team from all the bureaucracy and reporting that traditionally eat up company time. Meanwhile, the big company can take full advantage of the start-up's ideas, processes, culture, and technology.

Myth: Digital is about technology

Reality: It's about the customer

Managers often think that digital transformation is primarily about technology change. Of course technology change is involved—but smart companies realize that transformation is ultimately about better serving customer needs, whether through more-effective operations, mass customization, or new offers. Because digital enables—even demands—the connection of formerly siloed activities for this purpose, the company must often reorganize both people and technology.

In practice this may mean changing structure—for example, in situations where a more agile structure is merited, creating internal squads with the capabilities and authority necessary to follow projects from beginning to end. Although a squad is a team, it differs from most big-company teams in being empowered to solve key problems quickly, as an entrepreneur would.

The credit card giant Mastercard has a systematic process for building such squads, overseen by Mastercard Labs. Employees from various functional areas can submit ideas to qualify for three stage awards: Orange Box, Red Box, and Green Box. The Orange Box gives employees a chance to explore their ideas and pitch them. Recipients of this award receive a $1,000 prepaid card and coaching to develop a presentation about solving a specific customer problem. At the Red Box stage people turn an idea into a concept: The team receives $25,000 for testing, prototype development, and research and a 90-day guide outlining the steps needed to refine the concept. The Green Box was designed to create a commercialized product from an official incubation project inside the labs. At this stage team members leave their jobs for six months to work on the project.

One major global bank, ING, teaches an important lesson about getting such squads to work in more-traditional organizational structures. It recognized that to assign the right employees to cross-company initiatives, and to keep them from staying too long on an initiative that should be cut, it needed to support these intrapreneurs in transitioning between roles. It has developed a set of internal processes called PIE: P for *protect*, meaning that employees who leave their jobs to work on a squad project can return to those jobs if the initiative fails; I for *independence*, meaning that squad members have their own resources and can make their own decisions; and E for *encouragement*, meaning that if the squad is successful, its work will be widely celebrated in the company.

Of course, it must also be OK for these squads to fail. Failures, even relatively late ones, should not jeopardize a career. As ING CEO Ralph Hamers explains, "We have to be honest about failures. We also have to be honest about all that we learned in the process and that by using a different approach, we learned these lessons in a fraction of the time it takes competitors."

There's a framing aspect as well. As the Norwegian telecom giant Telenor (for which Nathan has done consulting) makes its digital transformation, it has experimented with job definitions. Instead of designating individuals as product owners—people who oversee functions and P&L—it now calls them project *managers*, responsible for designing the customer journey. This shift encourages them to operate like mini-CEOs, externally focused on the customer problem and able to work quickly across internal boundaries to deliver a solution.

Finally, it's important to recognize that transitioning to squads can be a painful process. In a radical example of such reorganization, ING eliminated divisions and functions and instead embraced an agile organizational structure with squads tasked to deliver improved customer journeys. When it reorganized, over a weekend, all the employees were fired and had to reapply for their jobs, through the lens of the customer need they solved. With the help of these and similar initiatives, ING plans to reduce its head count in the Netherlands and Belgium by 30%–40% over a five-year period. Not all transitions will be so dramatic, but in most cases some friction is inevitable when jobs are redefined.

Myth: Digital requires overhauling legacy systems

Reality: It's more often about incremental bridging

Digital transformation may ultimately require radically altering back-end legacy systems, but starting with a sweeping IT overhaul comes with great risks. Smart companies find a way to quickly develop front-end applications while slowly replacing their legacy systems in a modular, agile fashion. This can be achieved by building a middleware interface to connect the front and back ends, or by allowing business units to adopt needed solutions today while IT transforms the back end in an ambidextrous manner. Over time the pieces of the legacy system can be decommissioned, but progress in meeting customer needs doesn't have to wait until then.

For example, when TUI embarked on its digital transformation, it faced a difficult challenge: Its business operations in retail, telephone, and online were geographically and operationally separate, and back-end reservations systems in the UK were 35 years old. Technology was critical for the company at the time: The rise of Expedia and other OTA channels was threatening to totally disrupt the travel agency business. In this context it was very tempting for TUI to start its digital journey with a sweeping IT overhaul. But experience suggests that attempts to replace multiple complex, mission-critical systems all at once nearly always end in disaster. Instead, in the words of Jacky Simmonds, who was part of the leadership team, "the key was to envision the ideal customer journey and then see how it could make business sense through a digital lens."

Rather than embark on a complete overhaul, TUI developed a three-year plan to replace its technology, initially working with bespoke solutions to focus on a better customer experience. The company used this time to learn from customers what they wanted in a digital world. It then connected the front-end application to the legacy back end with a middleware interface. Next it divided the back end into modular subsystems and slowly replaced them, adding front-end functionality with each step. Every time the company upgraded a component of the back end or the front end, it first tested it in one market and then iterated the prototype to improve it before working with other business units.

Although TUI decided not to roll its reservations system out more broadly, given the diversity of its markets, a coherent digital strategy allowed the markets to work together, maximizing the investment in technology. The company has enjoyed a decade of steady growth throughout its digitization of the customer journey.

The bridging role of middleware interfaces is particularly apparent in the financial services sector. In 2015 the European Parliament adopted a new Directive on Payment Services (PSD2). One of the objectives of the legislation was to enable third-party developers to build applications and services around a financial institution. If an individual is unhappy with the bank's money-transfer fees, PSD2 makes it easier for that person to use alternative services provided by a third party. Instead of waiting to change the legacy infrastructure to address the challenges of PSD2, institutions such as Deutsche Bank and the Hungary-based OTP have focused on building APIs (application programming interfaces) that allow them to connect external providers, such as TransferWise and the AI-enabled wealth adviser Wealthify, to their legacy infrastructure.

We aren't suggesting that large companies can ignore the need to update legacy systems forever. However, postponing your digital transformation until you can update them fully or all at once is dangerous. If you break the problem into modules and create a middle-layer interface, you can maintain operational stability for the core of the organization while experimenting with satisfying customer needs.

For most companies, even those truly threatened by disruption, digital transformation is not usually about a root-and-branch reimagining of the value proposition or the business model. Rather, it is about both transforming the core using digital tools *and* discovering and capturing new opportunities enabled by digital. Each company we have described has incorporated different digital elements in its business model, and not all the changes were disruptive or intrusive. The keys to success have been a focus on customer needs, organizational flexibility, respect for incremental change, and awareness that new skills and technology must be not only acquired but also protected—something the best traditional companies have always been good at.

Originally published in July–August 2019. Reprint R1904F

What's Your Data Strategy?

by Leandro DalleMule and Thomas H. Davenport

MORE THAN EVER, the ability to manage torrents of data is critical to a company's success. But even with the emergence of data-management functions and chief data officers (CDOs), most companies remain badly behind the curve. Cross-industry studies show that on average, less than half of an organization's structured data is actively used in making decisions—and less than 1% of its unstructured data is analyzed or used at all. More than 70% of employees have access to data they should not, and 80% of analysts' time is spent simply discovering and preparing data. Data breaches are common, rogue data sets propagate in silos, and companies' data technology often isn't up to the demands put on it.

Having a CDO and a data-management function is a start, but neither can be fully effective in the absence of a coherent strategy for organizing, governing, analyzing, and deploying an organization's information assets. Indeed, without such strategic management many companies struggle to protect and leverage their data—and CDOs' tenures are often difficult and short (just 2.4 years on average, according to Gartner). In this article we describe a new framework for building a robust data strategy that can be applied across industries and levels of data maturity. The framework draws on our implementation experience at the global insurer AIG (where DalleMule is the CDO) and our study of half a dozen other large companies where its elements have been applied. The strategy enables superior data management and analytics—essential capabilities that support managerial decision making and ultimately enhance financial performance.

The "plumbing" aspects of data management may not be as sexy as the predictive models and colorful dashboards they produce, but they're vital to high performance. As such, they're not just the concern of the CIO and the CDO; ensuring smart data management is the responsibility of all C-suite executives, starting with the CEO.

Defense Versus Offense

Our framework addresses two key issues: It helps companies clarify the primary purpose of their data, and it guides them in strategic data management. Unlike other approaches we've seen, ours requires companies to make considered trade-offs between "defensive" and "offensive" uses of data and between control and flexibility in its use, as we describe below. Although information on enterprise data management is abundant, much of it is technical and focused on governance, best practices, tools, and the like. Few if any data-management frameworks are as business-focused as ours: It not only promotes the efficient use of data and allocation of resources but also helps companies design their data-management activities to support their overall strategy.

Data defense and offense are differentiated by distinct business objectives and the activities designed to address them. Data defense is about minimizing downside risk. Activities include ensuring compliance with regulations (such as rules governing data privacy and the integrity of financial reports), using analytics to detect and limit fraud, and building systems to prevent theft. Defensive efforts also ensure the integrity of data flowing through a company's internal systems by identifying, standardizing, and governing authoritative data sources, such as fundamental customer and supplier information or sales data, in a "single source of truth." Data offense focuses on supporting business objectives such as increasing revenue, profitability, and customer satisfaction. It typically includes activities that generate customer insights (data analysis and modeling,

Idea in Brief

The Challenge

To remain competitive, companies must wisely manage quantities of data. But data theft is common, flawed or duplicate data sets exist within organizations, and IT is often behind the curve.

The Solution

Companies need a coherent strategy that strikes the proper balance between two types of data

management: *defensive*, such as security and governance, and *offensive*, such as predictive analytics.

The Execution

Regardless of its industry, a company's data strategy is rarely static; typically, a chief data officer is in charge of ensuring that it dynamically adjusts as competitive pressures and overall corporate strategy shift.

for example) or integrate disparate customer and market data to support managerial decision making through, for instance, interactive dashboards.

Offensive activities tend to be most relevant for customer-focused business functions such as sales and marketing and are often more real-time than is defensive work, with its concentration on legal, financial, compliance, and IT concerns. (An exception would be data fraud protection, in which seconds count and real-time analytics smarts are critical.) Every company needs both offense and defense to succeed, but getting the balance right is tricky. In every organization we've talked with, the two compete fiercely for finite resources, funding, and people. As we shall see, putting equal emphasis on the two is optimal for some companies. But for many others it's wiser to favor one or the other.

Some company or environmental factors may influence the direction of data strategy: Strong regulation in an industry (financial services or health care, for example) would move the organization toward defense; strong competition for customers would shift it toward offense. The challenge for CDOs and the rest of the C-suite is to establish the appropriate trade-offs between defense and offense and to ensure the best balance in support of the company's overall strategy.

45

Decisions about these trade-offs are rooted in the fundamental dichotomy between standardizing data and keeping it more flexible. The more uniform data is, the easier it becomes to execute defensive processes, such as complying with regulatory requirements and implementing data-access controls. The more flexible data is—that is, the more readily it can be transformed or interpreted to meet specific business needs—the more useful it is in offense. Balancing offense and defense, then, requires balancing data control and flexibility, as we will describe.

Single Source, Multiple Versions

Before we explore the framework, it's important to distinguish between information and data and to differentiate information architecture from data architecture. According to Peter Drucker, information is "data endowed with relevance and purpose." Raw data, such as customer retention rates, sales figures, and supply costs, is of limited value until it has been integrated with other data and transformed into information that can guide decision making. Sales figures put into a historical or a market context suddenly have meaning—they may be climbing or falling relative to benchmarks or in response to a specific strategy.

A company's data architecture describes how data is collected, stored, transformed, distributed, and consumed. It includes the rules governing structured formats, such as databases and file systems, and the systems for connecting data with the business processes that consume it. Information architecture governs the processes and rules that convert data into useful information. For example, data architecture might feed raw daily advertising and sales data into information architecture systems, such as marketing dashboards, where it is integrated and analyzed to reveal relationships between ad spend and sales by channel and region.

Many organizations have attempted to create highly centralized, control-oriented approaches to data and information architectures. Previously known as information engineering and now as master data management, these top-down approaches are often

The elements of data strategy

	Defense	Offense
Key objectives	Ensure data security, privacy, integrity, quality, regulatory compliance, and governance	Improve competitive position and profitability
Core activities	Optimize data extraction, standardization, storage, and access	Optimize data analytics, modeling, visualization, transformation, and enrichment
Data-management orientation	Control	Flexibility
Enabling architecture	SSOT (Single source of truth)	MVOTs (Multiple versions of the truth)

not well suited to supporting a broad data strategy. Although they are effective for standardizing enterprise data, they can inhibit flexibility, making it harder to customize data or transform it into information that can be applied strategically. In our experience, a more flexible and realistic approach to data and information architectures involves both a single source of truth (SSOT) and multiple versions of the truth (MVOTs). The SSOT works at the data level; MVOTs support the management of information.

In the organizations we've studied, the concept of a single version of truth—for example, one inviolable primary source of revenue data—is fully grasped and accepted by IT and across the business. However, the idea that a single source can feed multiple versions of the truth (such as revenue figures that differ according to users' needs) is not well understood, commonly articulated, or, in general, properly executed.

The key innovation of our framework is this: It requires flexible data and information architectures that permit both single and multiple versions of the truth to support a defensive-offensive approach to data strategy.

A New Data Architecture Can Pay for Itself

WHEN COMPANIES LACK a robust SSOT-MVOTs data architecture, teams across the organization may create and store the data they need in siloed repositories that vary in depth, breadth, and formatting. Their data management is often done in isolation with inconsistent requirements. The process is inefficient and expensive and can result in the proliferation of multiple uncontrolled versions of the truth that aren't effectively reused. Because SSOTs and MVOTs concentrate, standardize, and streamline data-sourcing activities, they can dramatically cut operational costs.

One large financial services company doing business in more than 200 countries consolidated nearly 130 authoritative data sources, with trillions of records, into an SSOT. This allowed the company to rationalize its key data systems; eliminate much supporting IT infrastructure, such as databases and servers; and cut operating expenses by automating previously manual data consolidation. The automation alone yielded a 190% return on investment with a two-year payback time. Many companies will find that they can fund their entire data management programs, including staff salaries and technology costs, from the savings realized by consolidating data sources and decommissioning legacy systems.

The CDO and the data-management function should be fully responsible for building and operating the SSOT structure and using the savings it generates to fund the company's data program. Most important is to ensure at the outset that the SSOT addresses broad, high-priority business needs, such as applications that benefit customers or generate revenue, so that the project quickly yields results and savings—which encourages organization-wide buy-in.

OK. Let's parse that.

The SSOT is a logical, often virtual and cloud-based repository that contains one authoritative copy of all crucial data, such as customer, supplier, and product details. It must have robust data provenance and governance controls to ensure that the data can be relied on in defensive and offensive activities, and it must use a common language—not one that is specific to a particular business unit or function. Thus, for example, revenue is reported, customers are defined, and products are classified in a single, unchanging, agreed-upon way within the SSOT.

Not having an SSOT can lead to chaos. One large industrial company we studied had more than a dozen data sources containing similar supplier information, such as name and address. But the content was slightly different in each source. For example, one source identified a supplier as Acme; another called it Acme, Inc.; and a third labeled it ACME Corp. Meanwhile, various functions within the company were relying on differing data sources; often the functions weren't even aware that alternative sources existed. Human beings might be able to untangle such problems (though it would be labor-intensive), but traditional IT systems can't, so the company couldn't truly understand its relationship with the supplier. Fortunately, artificial intelligence tools that can sift through such data chaos to assemble an SSOT are becoming available. The industrial company ultimately tapped one and saved substantial IT costs by shutting down redundant systems. The SSOT allowed managers to identify suppliers that were selling to multiple business units within the company and to negotiate discounts. In the first year, having an SSOT yielded $75 million in benefits.

An SSOT is the source from which multiple versions of the truth are developed. MVOTs result from the business-specific transformation of data into information—data imbued with "relevance and purpose." Thus, as various groups within units or functions transform, label, and report data, they create distinct, controlled versions of the truth that, when queried, yield consistent, customized responses according to the groups' predetermined requirements.

Consider how a supplier might classify its clients Bayer and Apple according to industry. At the SSOT level these companies belong, respectively, to chemicals/pharmaceuticals and consumer electronics, and all data about the supplier's relationship with them, such as commercial transactions and market information, would be mapped accordingly. In the absence of MVOTs, the same would be true for all organizational purposes. But such broad industry classifications may be of little use to sales, for example, where a more practical version of the truth would classify Apple as a mobile phone or a laptop company, depending on which division sales was interacting with. Similarly, Bayer might be more usefully classified as a drug or a pesticide company for the purposes of competitive analysis. In short, multiple versions of the truth, derived from a common SSOT, support superior decision making.

Good Governance, Good Data

A SOUND DATA STRATEGY REQUIRES that the data contained in a company's single source of truth (SSOT) is of high quality, granular, and standardized, and that multiple versions of the truth (MVOTs) are carefully controlled and derived from the same SSOT. This necessitates good governance for both data and technology. In the absence of proper governance, some common problems arise:

- **Data definitions may be ambiguous and mutable.** With no concrete definition at the outset of what constitutes the "truth" (whether an SSOT or MVOTs), stakeholders will squander time and resources as they try to manage non standardized data.

- **Data rules are vague or inconsistently applied.** If rules for aggregating, integrating, and transforming data are unclear, misunderstood, or simply not followed—particularly when data transformation involves multiple poorly defined steps—it's difficult to reliably replicate transformations and leverage information across the organization.

- **Feedback loops for improving data transformation are absent.** Complex data analyses such as predictive modeling may be undertaken by one group but prove useful across an organization. Without mechanisms for making these outputs available to others (by, for example, integrating them into appropriate MVOTs), stakeholders may needlessly duplicate work or miss opportunities.

Strong data governance usually involves standing committees or review boards composed of business and technology executives, but it relies heavily on robust technology oversight. If technology rules prevent a marketing executive from buying a server on his or her corporate purchasing card, it's much less likely that marketing will, for instance, create unregulated "shadow" MVOTs or a marketing analytic that duplicates an existing one.

At a global asset management company we studied, the marketing and finance departments both produced monthly reports on television ad spending—MVOTs derived from a common SSOT. Marketing, interested in analyzing advertising effectiveness, reported on spending after ads had aired. Finance, focusing on cash flow, captured spending when invoices were paid. The reports therefore contained different numbers, but each represented an accurate version of the truth.

A Lake of Data

UNTIL A FEW YEARS AGO, technological limitations made it hard to build the SSOT-MVOTs data architecture needed to support a robust data strategy. Companies depended on traditional data warehouses that stored structured enterprise data in hierarchical files and folders, but these were not always suited to managing vast and growing volumes of data and new formats. To meet the need for a cheaper, more agile and scalable architecture, Silicon Valley engineers devised the "data lake," which can store virtually unlimited amounts of structured and unstructured data, from databases to spreadsheets to free text and image files. Data lakes are an ideal platform for SSOT-MVOTs architecture. A lake can house the SSOT, extracting, storing, and providing access to the organization's most granular data down to the level of individual transactions. And it can support the aggregation of SSOT data in nearly infinite ways in MVOTs that also reside in the lake. Data warehouses still have their uses: They store data for production applications (such as general ledger and order-management systems) that require tight security and access controls, which few data lakes can do. Many companies have both data lakes and warehouses, but the trend is for more and more data to reside in a lake.

Procter & Gamble has adopted a similar approach to data management. The company long had a centralized SSOT for all product and customer data, and other versions of data weren't allowed. But CDO Guy Peri and his team realized that the various business units had valid needs for customized interpretations of the data. The units are now permitted to create controlled data transformations for reporting that can be reliably mapped back to the SSOT. Thus the MVOTs diverge from the SSOT in consistent ways, and their provenance is clear.

In its application of the SSOT-MVOTs model, the Canadian Imperial Bank of Commerce (CIBC) automated processes to ensure that enterprise source data and data transformations remained aligned. CIBC's CDO, Jose Ribau, explains that the company's SSOT contains all basic client profile and preference data; MVOTs for loan origination and customer relationship management transform the source data into information that supports regulatory reporting and improved customer experience. Automated synchronization programs connect SSOT and MVOTs data, with nightly "exception handling" to identify and address data-integrity issues such as inconsistent customer profiles.

Although the SSOT-MVOTs model is conceptually straightforward, it requires robust data controls, standards, governance, and technology. Ideally, senior executives will actively participate on data governance boards and committees. But data governance isn't particularly fun. Typically, enterprise CDOs and CTOs lead data and technology governance processes, and business and technology managers in functions and units are the primary participants. What's critical is that single sources of the truth remain unique and valid, and that multiple versions of the truth diverge from the original source only in carefully controlled ways. (For more on data governance and technology, see the sidebars "Good Governance, Good Data" and "A Lake of Data.")

Striking a Balance

Let's return now to data strategy—striking the best balance between defense and offense and between control and flexibility. Whereas the CEO—often with the CIO—is ultimately responsible for a company's data strategy, the CDO commonly conceives it and leads its development and execution. The CDO must determine the right trade-offs while dynamically adjusting the balance by leveraging the SSOT and MVOTs architectures.

It's rare to find an organization—especially a large, complex one—in which data is both tightly controlled and flexibly used. With few exceptions, CDOs find that their best data strategy emphasizes either defense and control (which depends on a robust SSOT) or offense and flexibility (enabled by MVOTs). Devoting equal attention to offense and defense is sometimes optimal, but in general it's unwise to default to a 50/50 split rather than making considered, strategic trade-offs. To determine a company's current and desired positions on the offense-defense spectrum, the CDO must bear in mind, among other things, the company's overall strategy, its regulatory environment, the data capabilities of its competitors, the maturity of its data-management practices, and the size of its data budget. For example, insurance and financial services companies typically operate in heavily regulated environments, which argues for an emphasis on data defense. (That is the case at AIG.) Retailers, operating in a less-regulated environment where intense competition requires robust customer analytics, might emphasize offense. (See the exhibit "The data-strategy spectrum.")

As Peri points out, defense and offense often require differing approaches from IT and the data-management organization. Defense, he argues, is day-to-day and operational, and at P&G is largely overseen by permanent IT teams focused on master data management, information security, and so forth. Offense involves partnering with business leaders on tactical and strategic initiatives. Leaders may be reluctant to engage with master data management,

---

The data-strategy spectrum

A company's industry, competitive and regulatory environment, and overall strategy will inform its data strategy.

Hospitals operate in highly regulated environments where data quality and protection are paramount. They emphasize defense over offense.

Banks are heavily regulated and require strong data defense. But they operate in dynamic markets and so typically devote equal attention to data offense.

Retailers are less regulated, work with limited sensitive personal data, and must react rapidly to competition and market changes. They typically emphasize offense over defense.

Defense

Offense

Assess your strategy position

Choose from among the following 16 objectives the eight that are most important to your business. Selecting that subset will require considered trade-offs that reveal your offense-defense orientation.

	Check the eight that qualify.	Total number of checked boxes
1 Reduce general operating expenses		
2 Meet industry regulatory requirements		
3 Prevent cyberattacks and data breaches		
4 Mitigate operational risks such as poor access controls and data losses		
5 Improve IT infrastructure and reduce data-related costs		
6 Streamline back-office systems and processes		
7 Improve data quality (completeness, accuracy, timeliness)		
8 Rationalize multiple sources of data and information (consolidate and eliminate redundancy)		

Data defense
Strong defense is characterized by single source of truth (SSOT) architecture, robust data governance and controls, and a more centralized data-management organization.

	Data offense
	Data offense Strong offense is characterized by multiple versions of the truth (MVOTs) architecture, high data flexibility, and a more decentralized data-management organization.
9	Improve revenue through cross-selling, strategic pricing, and customer acquisition	
10	Create new products and services	
11	Respond rapidly to competitors and market changes	
12	Use sophisticated customer analytics to drive business results	
13	Leverage new sources of internal and external data	
14	Monetize company data (sell as a product or a service)	
15	Optimize existing strong bench of analysts and data scientists	
16	Generate return on investments in big data and analytics infrastructure	

but they are happy to collaborate on optimizing marketing and trade promotion spending.

Of course, plenty of cases don't fall neatly into either the offense or the defense category: The CDO of a large hedge fund told us that he was less concerned with data protection than with rapidly gathering and using new data. The most valuable data for his fund is primarily external, publicly or commercially available, captured in real time, and already of good quality, structured, and cleansed. Additionally, although his business is in financial services, it's not heavily regulated. Thus he focuses primarily on data offense. Wells Fargo's CDO, A. Charles Thomas, has enterprise responsibility for customer-related analytics, an offensive activity, and strives to keep the balance between offensive and defensive activities around 50/50, even structuring meeting agendas to focus equally on the two.

The tool "Assess your strategy position" offers diagnostic questions that can help CDOs place their companies on the offense-defense spectrum and gauge whether their data strategy aligns with their corporate strategy. Determining an organization's current and desired positions on the spectrum will force executives to make trade-offs between offensive and defensive investments. Of course, this tool is not a precise measure. CDOs should use the results to inform data strategy and discussions with other C-level executives.

We find that companies with the most-advanced data strategies started at one point and gradually migrated to a new, stable position. For example, they may have shifted their focus from defense and data control toward offense as their data defense matured or competition heated up. The opposite path—from offense toward defense, and from flexible toward controlled—is possible but usually more difficult.

Consider how data strategy has shifted at CIBC. The bank established the chief data officer role a few years ago and for the first 18 months maintained a 90% defensive orientation, focusing on governance, data standardization, and building new data-storage capabilities. When Jose Ribau took over as CDO, in 2015, he determined that CIBC's defense was sufficiently solid that he could shift toward offense, including more-advanced data modeling and data science work. Today CIBC's data strategy strikes a 50/50 balance. Ribau expects that the new attention to offense will drive increased ROI from data products and services and nurture analytical talent for the future.

Regardless of what industry a company is in, its position on the offense-defense spectrum is rarely static. As competitive pressure mounts, an insurer may decide to increase its focus on offensive activities. A hedge fund may find itself in a tougher regulatory environment that requires rebalancing its data strategy toward defense. How a company's data strategy changes in direction and velocity will be a function of its overall strategy, culture, competition, and market.

Organizing Data Management

As with most organizational design, data-management functions can be built centrally or decentralized by function or business unit. The optimal design will depend on a company's position on the offense-defense spectrum. A centralized data function typically has a single CDO with accountability across the entire organization, ensuring that data policies, governance, and standards are applied consistently. This design is most suitable for businesses that focus on data defense.

Conversely, several companies we studied found that data offense can be better executed through decentralized data management, typically with a CDO for each business unit and most corporate functions. "Unit CDOs" tend to report directly to their business but have a matrix reporting relationship to the enterprise CDO. That helps prevent the development of data silos (which can lead to redundant systems and duplicate work) and ensures that best practices are shared and standards are followed. Generally speaking, unit CDOs own their respective versions of the truth, while the enterprise CDO owns the SSOT. A decentralized approach is well suited to offensive strategies because it can increase the agility and customization of data reporting and analytics. In many companies, among them Wells

Fargo, CIBC, and P&G, the CDO is responsible for both analytics and data management, facilitating the ability to balance offense and defense.

Finally, in choosing between a centralized and a decentralized data function, it's important to consider how funding will be determined, allocated, and spent. The budget may appear larger for a centralized function than for a decentralized one simply because it's concentrated under one CDO. Decentralized budgets are typically more focused on offensive investments, are closer to the business users, and have more-tangible ROIs, whereas centralized budgets are more often focused on minimizing risk, reducing costs, and providing better data controls and regulatory oversight—activities that are less close to business users and usually have a less-tangible ROI. Thus creating a business case to justify the latter is usually trickier. The importance of investing in data governance and control—even if the payoff is abstract—is more easily understood and accepted if a company has suffered from a major regulatory challenge, a data breach, or some other serious defense-related issue. Absent a traumatic event, enterprise CDOs should spend time educating senior executives and their teams about data-defense principles and how they create value.

Emerging technologies may enable a next generation of data-management capabilities, potentially simplifying the implementation of defensive and offensive strategies. Machine learning, for example, is already facilitating the creation of a single source of truth in many companies we studied. The promise is more-dynamic, less-costly SSOTs and MVOTs. However, no new technology will obviate an effective, well-run data-management function. Our framework will become even more relevant as distributed technology solutions—blockchain, for example—come into play.

Data was once critical to only a few back-office processes, such as payroll and accounting. Today it is central to any business, and the importance of managing it strategically is only growing. In September 2016, according to the technology conglomerate

Cisco, global annual internet traffic surpassed one zettabyte (1021 bytes)—the equivalent, by one calculation, of 150 million years of high-definition video. It took 40 years to get to this point, but in the next four, data traffic will double. There is no avoiding the implications: Companies that have not yet built a data strategy and a strong data-management function need to catch up very fast or start planning for their exit.

Originally published in May–June 2017. Reprint R1703H

Competing in the Age of AI

by Marco Iansiti and Karim R. Lakhani

IN 2019, JUST FIVE YEARS after the Ant Financial Services Group was launched, the number of consumers using its services passed the one billion mark. Spun out of Alibaba, Ant Financial uses artificial intelligence and data from Alipay—its core mobile-payments platform—to run an extraordinary variety of businesses, including consumer lending, money market funds, wealth management, health insurance, credit-rating services, and even an online game that encourages people to reduce their carbon footprint. The company serves more than 10 times as many customers as the largest U.S. banks—with less than one-tenth the number of employees. At its last round of funding, in 2018, it had a valuation of $150 billion—almost half that of JPMorgan Chase, the world's most valuable financial-services company.

Unlike traditional banks, investment institutions, and insurance companies, Ant Financial is built on a digital core. There are no workers in its "critical path" of operating activities. AI runs the show. There is no manager approving loans, no employee providing financial advice, no representative authorizing consumer medical expenses. And without the operating constraints that limit traditional firms, Ant Financial can compete in unprecedented ways and achieve unbridled growth and impact across a variety of industries.

The age of AI is being ushered in by the emergence of this new kind of firm. Ant Financial's cohort includes giants like Google,

61

Facebook, Alibaba, and Tencent, and many smaller, rapidly growing firms, from Zebra Medical Vision and Wayfair to Indigo Ag and Ocado. Every time we use a service from one of those companies, the same remarkable thing happens: Rather than relying on traditional business processes operated by workers, managers, process engineers, supervisors, or customer service representatives, the value we get is served up by algorithms. Microsoft's CEO, Satya Nadella, refers to AI as the new "runtime" of the firm. True, managers and engineers design the AI and the software that makes the algorithms work, but after that, the system delivers value on its own, through digital automation or by leveraging an ecosystem of providers outside the firm. AI sets the prices on Amazon, recommends songs on Spotify, matches buyers and sellers on Indigo's marketplace, and qualifies borrowers for an Ant Financial loan.

The elimination of traditional constraints transforms the rules of competition. As digital networks and algorithms are woven into the fabric of firms, industries begin to function differently and the lines between them blur. The changes extend well beyond born-digital firms, as more-traditional organizations, confronted by new rivals, move toward AI-based models too. Walmart, Fidelity, Honeywell, and Comcast are now tapping extensively into data, algorithms, and digital networks to compete convincingly in this new era. Whether you're leading a digital start-up or working to revamp a traditional enterprise, it's essential to understand the revolutionary impact AI has on operations, strategy, and competition.

The AI Factory

At the core of the new firm is a decision factory—what we call the "AI factory." Its software runs the millions of daily ad auctions at Google and Baidu. Its algorithms decide which cars offer rides on Didi, Grab, Lyft, and Uber. It sets the prices of headphones and polo shirts on Amazon and runs the robots that clean floors in some Walmart locations. It enables customer service bots at Fidelity and interprets X-rays at Zebra Medical. In each case the AI factory treats decision-making as a science. Analytics systematically convert internal and

Idea in Brief

The Market Change

We're seeing the emergence of a new kind of firm—one in which artificial intelligence is the main source of value creation and delivery.

The Challenge

The AI-driven operating model is blurring the lines that used to

separate industries and is upending the rules of business competition.

The Upshot

For digital start-ups and traditional firms alike, it's essential to understand the revolutionary impact AI has on operations, strategy, and competition.

---

external data into predictions, insights, and choices, which in turn guide and automate operational workflows.

Oddly enough, the AI that can drive the explosive growth of a digital firm often isn't even all that sophisticated. To bring about dramatic change, AI doesn't need to be the stuff of science fiction— indistinguishable from human behavior or simulating human reasoning, a capability sometimes referred to as "strong AI." You need only a computer system to be able to perform tasks traditionally handled by people—what is often referred to as "weak AI."

With weak AI, the AI factory can already take on a range of critical decisions. In some cases it might manage information businesses (such as Google and Facebook). In other cases it will guide how the company builds, delivers, or operates actual physical products (like Amazon's warehouse robots or Waymo, Google's self-driving car service). But in all cases digital decision factories handle some of the most critical processes and operating decisions. Software makes up the core of the firm, while humans are moved to the edge.

Four components are essential to every factory. The first is the data pipeline, the semiautomated process that gathers, cleans, integrates, and safeguards data in a systematic, sustainable, and scalable way. The second is algorithms, which generate predictions about future states or actions of the business. The third is an experimentation platform, on which hypotheses regarding new algorithms are tested to ensure that their suggestions are having the intended effect. The fourth is infrastructure, the systems that embed this process in software and connect it to internal and external users.

Take a search engine like Google or Bing. As soon as someone starts to type a few letters into the search box, algorithms dynamically predict the full search term on the basis of terms that many users have typed in before and this particular user's past actions. These predictions are captured in a drop-down menu (the "autosuggest box") that helps the user zero in quickly on a relevant search. Every keystroke and every click are captured as data points, and every data point improves the predictions for future searches. AI also generates the organic search results, which are drawn from a previously assembled index of the web and optimized according to the clicks generated on the results of previous searches. The entry of the term also sets off an automated auction for the ads most relevant to the user's search, the results of which are shaped by additional experimentation and learning loops. Any click on or away from the search query or search results page provides useful data. The more searches, the better the predictions, and the better the predictions, the more the search engine is used.

Removing Limits to Scale, Scope, and Learning

The concept of scale has been central in business since at least the Industrial Revolution. The great Alfred Chandler described how modern industrial firms could reach unprecedented levels of production at much lower unit cost, giving large firms an important edge over smaller rivals. He also highlighted the benefits companies could reap from the ability to achieve greater production scope, or variety. The push for improvement and innovation added a third requirement for firms: learning. Scale, scope, and learning have come to be considered the essential drivers of a firm's operating performance. And for a long time they've been enabled by carefully defined business processes that rely on labor and management to deliver products and services to customers—and that are reinforced by traditional IT systems.

After hundreds of years of incremental improvements to the industrial model, the digital firm is now radically changing the scale, scope, and learning paradigm. AI-driven processes can be scaled up much more rapidly than traditional processes can, allow for much greater scope because they can easily be connected with other digitized businesses, and create incredibly powerful opportunities for learning and improvement—like the ability to produce ever more accurate and sophisticated customer-behavior models and then tailor services accordingly.

In traditional operating models, scale inevitably reaches a point at which it delivers diminishing returns. But we don't necessarily see this with AI-driven models, in which the return on scale can continue to climb to previously unheard-of levels. (See the exhibit "How AI-driven companies can outstrip traditional firms.") Now imagine what happens when an AI-driven firm competes with a traditional firm by serving the same customers with a similar (or better) value proposition and a much more scalable operating model.

How AI-driven companies can outstrip traditional firms

The value that scale delivers eventually tapers off in traditional operating models, but in digital operating models, it can climb much higher.

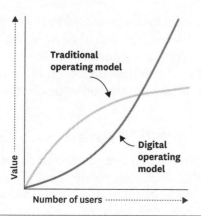

We call this kind of confrontation a "collision." As both learning and network effects amplify volume's impact on value creation, firms built on a digital core can overwhelm traditional organizations. Consider the outcome when Amazon collides with traditional retailers, Ant Financial with traditional banks, and Didi and Uber with traditional taxi services. As Clayton Christensen, Michael Raynor, and Rory McDonald argued in "What Is Disruptive Innovation?" (HBR, December 2015), such competitive upsets don't fit the disruption model. Collisions are not caused by a particular innovation in a technology or a business model. They're the result of the emergence of a completely different kind of firm. And they can fundamentally alter industries and reshape the nature of competitive advantage.

Note that it can take quite a while for AI-driven operating models to generate economic value anywhere near the value that traditional operating models generate at scale. Network effects produce little value before they reach critical mass, and most newly applied algorithms suffer from a "cold start" before acquiring adequate data. Ant Financial grew rapidly, but its core payment service, Alipay, which had been launched in 2004 by Alibaba, took years to reach its current volume. This explains why executives ensconced in the traditional model have a difficult time at first believing that the digital model will ever catch up. But once the digital operating model really gets going, it can deliver far superior value and quickly overtake traditional firms.

Collisions between AI-driven and traditional firms are happening across industries: software, financial services, retail, telecommunications, media, health care, automobiles, and even agribusiness. It's hard to think of a business that isn't facing the pressing need to digitize its operating model and respond to the new threats.

Rebuilding Traditional Enterprises

For leaders of traditional firms, competing with digital rivals involves more than deploying enterprise software or even building data pipelines, understanding algorithms, and experimenting. It requires rearchitecting the firm's organization and operating model.

For a very, very long time, companies have optimized their scale, scope, and learning through greater focus and specialization, which led to the siloed structures that the vast majority of enterprises today have. Generations of information technology didn't change this pattern. For decades, IT was used to enhance the performance of specific functions and organizational units. Traditional enterprise systems often even reinforced silos and the divisions across functions and products.

Silos, however, are the enemy of AI-powered growth. Indeed, businesses like Google Ads and Ant Financial's MyBank deliberately forgo them and are designed to leverage an integrated core of data and a unified, consistent code base. When each silo in a firm has its own data and code, internal development is fragmented, and it's nearly impossible to build connections across the silos or with external business networks or ecosystems. It's also nearly impossible to develop a 360-degree understanding of the customer that both serves and draws from every department and function. So when firms set up a new digital core, they should avoid creating deep organizational divisions within it.

While the transition to an AI-driven model is challenging, many traditional firms—some of which we've worked with—have begun to make the shift. In fact, in a recent study we looked at more than 350 traditional enterprises in both service and manufacturing sectors and found that the majority had started building a greater focus on data and analytics into their organizations. Many—including Nordstrom, Vodafone, Comcast, and Visa—had already made important inroads, digitizing and redesigning key components of their operating models and developing sophisticated data platforms and AI capabilities. You don't have to be a software start-up to digitize critical elements of your business—but you do have to confront silos and fragmented legacy systems, add capabilities, and retool your culture. (For a closer look at the key principles that should drive such transformations, see the sidebar "Putting AI at the Firm's Core.")

Fidelity Investments is using AI to enable processes in important areas, including customer service, customer insights, and investment

Putting AI at the Firm's Core

THE TRANSITION FROM A TRADITIONAL firm to an AI-driven organization cannot happen in a skunkworks or be spearheaded by some separate autonomous group. It requires a holistic effort. In our research and our work with a variety of companies, we've come up with five principles that should guide transformations (beyond common best practices for leading change):

One Strategy

Rearchitecting a company's operating model means rebuilding each business unit on a new, integrated foundation of data, analytics, and software. This challenging and time-consuming undertaking demands focus and a consistent top-down mandate to coordinate and inspire the many bottom-up efforts involved.

A Clear Architecture

A new approach based on data, analytics, and AI requires some centralization and a lot of consistency. Data assets should be integrated across a range of applications to maximize their impact. Fragmented data will be virtually impossible to safeguard consistently, especially given privacy and security considerations. If the data isn't all held in centralized repositories, then the organization must at least have an accurate catalog of where the data is, explicit guidelines for what to do with it (and how to protect it), and standards for when and how to store it so that it can be used and reused by multiple parties.

The Right Capabilities

Though building a base of software, data science, and advanced analytics capabilities will take time, much can be done with a small number of moti-

recommendations. Its AI initiatives build on a multiyear effort to integrate data assets into one digital core and redesign the organization around it. The work is by no means finished, but the impact of AI is already evident in many high-value use cases across the company. To take on Amazon, Walmart is rebuilding its operating model around AI and replacing traditional siloed enterprise software systems with an integrated, cloud-based architecture. That will allow Walmart to use its unique data assets in a variety of powerful new applications and automate or enhance a growing number of oper-

vated, knowledgeable people. However, many organizations fail to realize that they need to systematically hire a very different kind of talent and set up career paths and incentive systems for those employees.

An Agile "Product" Focus

Building an AI-centric operating model is about taking traditional processes and transforming them into software. Developing a product-focused mentality is essential to getting this done. Like the product managers at any world-class software development project, the IT teams deploying AI-centered applications should have a deep understanding of the use cases they're enabling—a product management orientation that goes well beyond the approach of traditional IT organizations. In the past, IT was largely about keeping old systems working, deploying software updates, protecting against cyberattacks, and running help desks. Developing operating-model software is a different game.

Multidisciplinary Governance

The governance of digital assets has become increasingly important and complex and calls for well-thought-out collaboration across disparate disciplines and functions. The challenges of data privacy, algorithmic bias, and cybersecurity are increasing risk and even government intervention and regulation. Governance should integrate a legal and corporate affairs function, which may even be involved in product and technology decisions. AI requires deep thinking about legal and ethical challenges, including careful consideration of what data should be stored and preserved (and what data should not).

ating tasks with AI and analytics. At Microsoft, Nadella is betting the company's future on a wholesale transformation of its operating model. (See the sidebar "Microsoft's AI Transformation.")

Rethinking Strategy and Capabilities

As AI-powered firms collide with traditional businesses, competitive advantage is increasingly defined by the ability to shape and control digital networks. (See "Why Some Platforms Thrive and Others

Microsoft's AI Transformation

MICROSOFT'S TRANSFORMATION INTO AN AI-DRIVEN firm took years of research but gained steam with the reorganization of its internal IT and data assets, which had been dispersed across the company's various operations. That effort was led by Kurt DelBene, the former head of Microsoft's Office business, who'd left to help fix the U.S. government's HealthCare.gov site before returning to Microsoft in 2015.

There's a reason that CEO Satya Nadella chose someone with product experience to run IT and build the "AI factory" that would be the foundation of the firm's new operating model. "Our product is the process," DelBene told us. "First, we are going to articulate what the vision should be for the systems and processes we support. Second, we're going to be run like a product development team. And we're going to be agile-based." To strengthen that orientation on his team, he brought in handpicked leaders and engineers from the product functions.

Today Core Engineering—as the IT operation is now known—is a showcase for Microsoft's own transformation. Thanks to the group's work, many traditional processes that used to be performed in silos are enabled by one consistent software base residing in Microsoft's Azure cloud. In addition, the team is driving toward a common data architecture across the company. The new, AI-based operating platform connects the sprawling organization with a shared software-component library, algorithm repository, and data catalog, all used to rapidly enable and deploy digital processes across different lines of business.

Beyond increasing productivity and scalability, the AI also helps head off problems. "We leverage AI to know when things are starting to behave in unexpected ways," DelBene says. "The best we could do in the past is react as fast as possible. Now we can preempt things, from bad contracts to cyberbreaches."

Don't," HBR, January–February 2019.) Organizations that excel at connecting businesses, aggregating the data that flows among them, and extracting its value through analytics and AI will have the upper hand. Traditional network effects and AI-driven learning curves will reinforce each other, multiplying each other's impact. You can see this dynamic in companies such as Google, Facebook, Tencent, and Alibaba, which have become powerful "hub" firms by accumulating data through their many network connections and building the algorithms necessary to heighten competitive advantages across disparate industries.

Meanwhile, conventional approaches to strategy that focus on traditional industry analysis are becoming increasingly ineffective. Take automotive companies. They're facing a variety of new digital threats, from Uber to Waymo, each coming from outside traditional industry boundaries. But if auto executives think of cars beyond their traditional industry context, as a highly connected, AI-enabled service, they can not only defend themselves but also unleash new value—through local commerce opportunities, ads, news and entertainment feeds, location-based services, and so on.

The advice to executives was once to stick with businesses they knew, in industries they understood. But synergies in algorithms and data flows do not respect industry boundaries. And organizations that can't leverage customers and data across those boundaries are likely to be at a big disadvantage. Instead of focusing on industry analysis and on the management of companies' internal resources, strategy needs to focus on the connections firms create across industries and the flow of data through the networks the firms use.

All this has major implications for organizations and their employees. Machine learning will transform the nature of almost every job, regardless of occupation, income level, or specialization. Undoubtedly, AI-based operating models can exact a real human toll. Several studies suggest that perhaps half of current work activities may be replaced by AI-enabled systems. We shouldn't be too surprised by that. After all, operating models have long been designed to make many tasks predictable and repeatable. Processes for scanning products at checkout, making lattes, and removing hernias, for instance, benefit from standardization and don't require too much human creativity. While AI improvements will enrich many jobs and generate a variety of interesting opportunities, it seems inevitable that they will also cause widespread dislocation in many occupations.

The dislocations will include not only job replacement but also the erosion of traditional capabilities. In almost every setting, AI-powered firms are taking on highly specialized organizations. In an AI-driven world, the requirements for competition have less to do with specialization and more to do with a universal set of capabilities in data sourcing, processing, analytics, and algorithm development. These new universal capabilities are reshaping strategy, business design, and even leadership. Strategies in very diverse digital and networked businesses now look similar, as do the drivers of operating performance. Industry expertise has become less critical. When Uber looked for a new CEO, the board hired someone who had previously run a digital firm—Expedia—not a limousine services company.

We're moving from an era of core competencies that differ from industry to industry to an age shaped by data and analytics and powered by algorithms—all hosted in the cloud for anyone to use. This is why Alibaba and Amazon are able to compete in industries as disparate as retail and financial services, and health care and credit scoring. These sectors now have many similar technological foundations and employ common methods and tools. Strategies are shifting away from traditional differentiation based on cost, quality, and brand equity and specialized, vertical expertise and toward advantages like business network position, the accumulation of unique data, and the deployment of sophisticated analytics.

The Leadership Challenge

Though it can unleash enormous growth, the removal of operating constraints isn't always a good thing. Frictionless systems are prone to instability and hard to stop once they're in motion. Think of a car without brakes or a skier who can't slow down. A digital signal—a viral meme, for instance—can spread rapidly through networks and can be just about impossible to halt, even for the organization that launched it in the first place or an entity that controls the key hubs in a network. Without friction, a video inciting violence or a phony or manipulative headline can quickly spread to billions of people on a variety of networks, even morphing to optimize click-throughs and downloads. If you have a message to send, AI offers a fantastic way to reach vast numbers of people and personalize that message for them. But the marketer's paradise can be a citizen's nightmare.

Digital operating models can aggregate harm along with value. Even when the intent is positive, the potential downside can be significant. A mistake can expose a large digital network to a destructive cyberattack. Algorithms, if left unchecked, can exacerbate bias and misinformation on a massive scale. Risks can be greatly magnified. Consider the way that digital banks are aggregating consumer savings in an unprecedented fashion. Ant Financial, which now operates one of the largest money market funds in the world, is entrusted with the savings of hundreds of millions of Chinese consumers. The risks that presents are significant, especially for a relatively unproven institution.

Digital scale, scope, and learning create a slew of new challenges—not just privacy and cybersecurity problems, but social turbulence resulting from market concentration, dislocations, and increased inequality. The institutions designed to keep an eye on business—regulatory bodies, for example—are struggling to keep up with all the rapid change.

In an AI-driven world, once an offering's fit with a market is ensured, user numbers, engagement, and revenues can skyrocket. Yet it's increasingly obvious that unconstrained growth is dangerous. The potential for businesses that embrace digital operating models is huge, but the capacity to inflict widespread harm needs to be explicitly considered. Navigating these opportunities and threats will be a real test of leadership for both businesses and public institutions.

Originally published in January–February 2020. Reprint R2001C

Building the AI-Powered Organization

by Tim Fountaine, Brian McCarthy, and Tamim Saleh

ARTIFICIAL INTELLIGENCE IS reshaping business—though not at the blistering pace many assume. True, AI is now guiding decisions on everything from crop harvests to bank loans, and once pie-in-the-sky prospects such as totally automated customer service are on the horizon. The technologies that enable AI, like development platforms and vast processing power and data storage, are advancing rapidly and becoming increasingly affordable. The time seems ripe for companies to capitalize on AI. Indeed, we estimate that AI will add $13 trillion to the global economy over the next decade.

Yet, despite the promise of AI, many organizations' efforts with it are falling short. We've surveyed thousands of executives about how their companies use and organize for AI and advanced analytics, and our data shows that only 8% of firms engage in core practices that support widespread adoption. Most firms have run only ad hoc pilots or are applying AI in just a single business process.

Why the slow progress? At the highest level, it's a reflection of a failure to rewire the organization. In our surveys and our work with hundreds of clients, we've seen that AI initiatives face formidable cultural and organizational barriers. But we've also seen that leaders who at the outset take steps to break down those barriers can effectively capture AI's opportunities.

Making the Shift

One of the biggest mistakes leaders make is to view AI as a plug-and-play technology with immediate returns. Deciding to get a few projects up and running, they begin investing millions in data infrastructure, AI software tools, data expertise, and model development. Some of the pilots manage to eke out small gains in pockets of organizations. But then months or years pass without bringing the big wins executives expected. Firms struggle to move from the pilots to companywide programs—and from a focus on discrete business problems, such as improved customer segmentation, to big business challenges, like optimizing the entire customer journey.

Leaders also often think too narrowly about AI requirements. While cutting-edge technology and talent are certainly needed, it's equally important to align a company's culture, structure, and ways of working to support broad AI adoption. But at most businesses that aren't born digital, traditional mindsets and ways of working run counter to those needed for AI.

To scale up AI, companies must make three shifts:

From siloed work to interdisciplinary collaboration

AI has the biggest impact when it's developed by cross-functional teams with a mix of skills and perspectives. Having business and operational people work side by side with analytics experts will ensure that initiatives address broad organizational priorities, not just isolated business issues. Diverse teams can also think through the operational changes new applications may require—they're likelier to recognize, say, that the introduction of an algorithm that predicts maintenance needs should be accompanied by an overhaul of maintenance workflows. And when development teams involve end users in the design of applications, the chances of adoption increase dramatically.

Idea in Brief

The Problem

Many companies' efforts to scale up artificial intelligence fall short. That's because only 8% of firms are engaging in core practices that support widespread adoption.

The Solution

Cutting-edge technology and talent are not enough. Companies must break down organizational and cultural barriers that stand in AI's way.

The Leadership Imperatives

Leaders must convey the urgency of AI initiatives and their benefits for all; spend at least as much on adoption as on technology; organize AI work on the basis of the company's AI maturity, business complexity, and innovation pace; and invest in AI education for everyone.

From experience-based, leader-driven decision making to data-driven decision making at the front line

When AI is adopted broadly, employees up and down the hierarchy will augment their own judgment and intuition with algorithms' recommendations to arrive at better answers than either humans or machines could reach on their own. But for this approach to work, people at all levels have to trust the algorithms' suggestions and feel empowered to make decisions—and that means abandoning the traditional top-down approach. If employees have to consult a higher-up before taking action, that will inhibit the use of AI.

Decision processes shifted dramatically at one organization when it replaced a complex manual method for scheduling events with a new AI system. Historically, the firm's event planners had used colored tags, pins, and stickers to track conflicts, participants' preferences, and other considerations. They'd often relied on gut instinct and on input from senior managers, who also were operating on their instincts, to make decisions. The new system rapidly analyzed the vast range of scheduling permutations, using first one algorithm to distill hundreds of millions of options into millions of scenarios, and then another algorithm to boil down those millions into just hundreds, ranking the optimal schedules for each participant. Experienced human planners then applied their expertise to make final decisions supported by the data, without the need to get input from their leaders. The planners adopted the tool readily, trusting its output because they'd helped set its parameters and constraints and knew that they themselves would make the final call.

From rigid and risk-averse to agile, experimental, and adaptable

Organizations must shed the mindset that an idea needs to be fully baked or a business tool must have every bell and whistle before it's deployed. On the first iteration, AI applications rarely have all their desired functionality. A test-and-learn mentality will reframe mistakes as a source of discoveries, reducing the fear of failure. Getting early user feedback and incorporating it into the next version will allow firms to correct minor issues before they become costly problems. Development will speed up, enabling small AI teams to create minimum viable products in a matter of weeks rather than months.

Such fundamental shifts don't come easily. They require leaders to prepare, motivate, and equip the workforce to make a change. But leaders must first be prepared themselves. We've seen failure after failure caused by the lack of a foundational understanding of AI among senior executives. (Further on, we'll discuss how analytics academies can help leaders acquire that understanding.)

Setting Up for Success

To get employees on board and smooth the way for successful AI launches, leaders should devote early attention to several tasks:

Explaining why

A compelling story helps organizations understand the urgency of change initiatives and how all will benefit from them. This is particularly critical with AI projects, because fear that AI will take away jobs increases employees' resistance to it.

Leaders have to provide a vision that rallies everyone around a common goal. Workers must understand why AI is important to the business and how they'll fit into a new, AI-oriented culture. In particular, they need reassurance that AI will enhance rather than diminish or even eliminate their roles. (Our research shows that the majority of workers will need to adapt to using AI rather than be replaced by AI.)

When a large retail conglomerate wanted to get its employees behind its AI strategy, management presented it as an existential imperative. Leaders described the threat that digital retailers posed and how AI could help fend it off by improving the firm's operational efficiency and responsiveness. By issuing a call to arms in a fight for survival, management underscored the critical role that employees had to play.

In sharing their vision, the company's leaders put a spotlight on workers who had piloted a new AI tool that helped them optimize stores' product assortments and increase revenue. That inspired other workers to imagine how AI could augment and elevate their performance.

Anticipating unique barriers to change

Some obstacles, such as workers' fear of becoming obsolete, are common across organizations. But a company's culture may also have distinctive characteristics that contribute to resistance. For example, if a company has relationship managers who pride themselves on being attuned to customer needs, they may reject the notion that a machine could have better ideas about what customers want and ignore an AI tool's tailored product recommendations. And managers in large organizations who believe their status is based on the number of people they oversee might object to the decentralized decision making or reduction in reports that AI could allow.

In other cases, siloed processes can inhibit the broad adoption of AI. Organizations that assign budgets by function or business unit may struggle to assemble interdisciplinary agile teams, for example.

Some solutions can be found by reviewing how past change initiatives overcame barriers. Others may involve aligning AI initiatives with the very cultural values that seem like obstacles. At one financial institution with a strong emphasis on relationship banking, for example, leaders highlighted AI's ability to enhance ties with customers. The bank created a booklet for relationship managers that showed how combining their expertise and skills with AI's tailored product recommendations could improve customers' experiences and increase revenue and profit. The AI adoption program also included a contest for sales conversions driven by using the new tool; the winners' achievements were showcased in the CEO's monthly newsletter to employees.

A relatively new class of expert, analytics translators, can play a role in identifying roadblocks. These people bridge the data engineers and scientists from the technical realm with the people from the business realm—marketing, supply chain, manufacturing, risk personnel, and so on. Translators help ensure that the AI applications developed address business needs and that adoption goes smoothly. Early in the implementation process, they may survey end users, observe their habits, and study workflows to diagnose and fix problems.

Understanding the barriers to change can not only inform leaders about how to communicate with the workforce but also help them determine where to invest, what AI initiatives are most feasible, what training should be offered, what incentives may be necessary, and more.

Budgeting as much for integration and adoption as for technology (if not more)

In one of our surveys nearly 90% of the companies that had engaged in successful scaling practices had spent more than half of their analytics budgets on activities that drove adoption, such as workflow redesign, communication, and training. Only 23% of the remaining companies had committed similar resources.

Consider one telecom provider that was launching a new AI-driven customer-retention program in its call center. The company invested simultaneously in AI model development and in helping the center's employees transition to the new approach. Instead of just reacting to calls canceling service, they would proactively reach out to customers at risk of defection, giving them AI-generated recommendations on new offers they'd be likely to accept. The employees got training and on-the-job coaching in the sales skills needed to close the business. Coaches and managers listened in on their calls, gave them individualized feedback, and continually updated the training materials and call scripts. Thanks to those coordinated efforts, the new program reduced customer attrition by 10%.

Balancing feasibility, time investment, and value

Pursuing initiatives that are unduly difficult to implement or require more than a year to launch can sabotage both current and future AI projects.

Organizations needn't focus solely on quick wins; they should develop a portfolio of initiatives with different time horizons. Automated processes that don't need human intervention, such as AI-assisted fraud detection, can deliver a return in months, while projects that require human involvement, such as AI-supported customer service, are likely to pay off over a longer period. Prioritization should be based on a long-term (typically three-year) view and take into consideration how several initiatives with different time lines could be combined to maximize value. For example, to achieve a view of customers detailed enough to allow AI to do microsegmentation, a company might need to set up a number of sales and marketing initiatives. Some, such as targeted offers, might deliver value in a few months, while it might take 12 to 18 months for the entire suite of capabilities to achieve full impact.

An Asian Pacific retailer determined that an AI initiative to optimize floor space and inventory placement wouldn't yield its complete value unless the company refurbished all its stores, reallocating the space for each category of goods. After much debate, the firm's executives decided the project was important enough to future profitability to proceed—but not without splitting it in two. Part one produced an AI tool that gave store managers recommendations for a few incremental items that would sell well in their outlets. The tool provided only a small fraction of the total return anticipated, but the managers could get the new items into stores immediately, demonstrating the project's benefits and building enthusiasm for the multiyear journey ahead.

Organizing for Scale

There's a lot of debate about where AI and analytics capabilities should reside within organizations. Often leaders simply ask, "What organizational model works best?" and then, after hearing what succeeded at other companies, do one of three things: consolidate the majority of AI and analytics capabilities within a central "hub"; decentralize them and embed them mostly in the business units ("the spokes"); or distribute them across both, using a hybrid ("hub-and-spoke") model. We've found that none of these models is always better than the others at getting AI up to scale; the right choice depends on a firm's individual situation.

Consider two large financial institutions we've worked with. One consolidated its AI and analytics teams in a central hub, with all analytics staff reporting to the chief data and analytics officer and being deployed to business units as needed. The second decentralized nearly all its analytics talent, having teams reside in and report to the business units. Both firms developed AI on a scale at the top of their industry; the second organization grew from 30 to 200 profitable AI initiatives in just two years. And both selected their model after taking into account their organizations' structure, capabilities, strategy, and unique characteristics.

The hub

A small handful of responsibilities are always best handled by a hub and led by the chief analytics or chief data officer. These include data governance, AI recruiting and training strategy, and work with third-party providers of data and AI services and software. Hubs should nurture AI talent, create communities where AI experts can share best practices, and lay out processes for AI development across the organization. Our research shows that companies that have implemented AI on a large scale are three times as likely as their peers to have a hub and 2.5 times as likely to have a clear methodology for creating models, interpreting insights, and deploying new AI capabilities.

Hubs should also be responsible for systems and standards related to AI. These should be driven by the needs of a firm's initiatives, which means they should be developed gradually, rather than set up in one fell swoop, before business cases have been determined. We've seen many organizations squander significant time and money—spending hundreds of millions of dollars—up front on companywide data-cleaning and data-integration projects, only to abort those efforts midway, realizing little or no benefits.

In contrast, when a European bank found that conflicting data-management strategies were hindering its development of new AI tools, it took a slower approach, making a plan to unify its data architecture and management over the next four years as it built various business cases for its AI transformation. This multiphase program, which also includes an organizational redesign and a revised talent strategy, is expected to have an annual impact of more than $900 million.

The spokes

Another handful of responsibilities should almost always be owned by the spokes, because they're closest to those who will be using the AI systems. Among them are tasks related to adoption, including end-user training, workflow redesign, incentive programs, performance management, and impact tracking.

To encourage customers to embrace the AI-enabled services offered with its smart, connected equipment, one manufacturer's sales and service organization created a "SWAT team" that supported customers using the product and developed a pricing plan to boost adoption. Such work is clearly the bailiwick of a spoke and can't be delegated to an analytics hub.

The gray area

Much of the work in successful AI transformations falls into a gray area in terms of responsibility. Key tasks—setting the direction for AI projects, analyzing the problems they'll solve, building the algorithms, designing the tools, testing them with end users, managing the change, and creating the supporting IT infrastructure—can be owned by either the hub or the spoke, shared by both, or shared with IT. (See the exhibit "Organizing AI for scale.") Deciding where

Organizing AI for scale

AI-enabled companies divide key roles between a hub and spokes. A few tasks are always owned by the hub, and the spokes always own execution. The rest of the work falls into a gray area, and a firm's individual characteristics determine where it should be done.

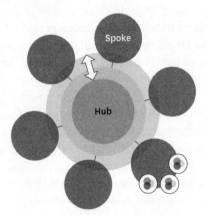

Governing coalition
A team of business, IT, and analytics leaders that
share accountability for the AI transformation

Hub
A central group headed by a C-level analytics executive who aligns strategy

Responsibilities
- Talent recruitment and training strategy
- Performance management
- Partnerships with providers of data and AI services and software
- AI standards, processes, policies

Gray area
Work that could be owned by the hub or spokes or shared with IT

Responsibilities
- Project direction, delivery, change management
- Data strategy, data architecture, code development
- User experience
- IT infrastructure
- Organizational capability assessment, strategy, funding

Spoke
A business unit, function, or geography, which assigns a manager to be the AI product owner and a business analyst to assist him or her

Responsibilities
- Oversight of execution teams
- Solution adoption
- Performance tracking

Execution teams
Assembled from the hub, spoke, and gray area for the duration of the project

Key roles
- Product owner
- Analytics translator
- Data scientist
- Data engineer
- Data architect
- Visualization specialist
- UI designer
- Business analyst

responsibility should lie within an organization is not an exact science, but it should be influenced by three factors:

The maturity of AI capabilities. When a company is early in its AI journey, it often makes sense for analytics executives, data scientists, data engineers, user interface designers, visualization specialists who graphically interpret analytics findings, and the like to sit within a hub and be deployed as needed to the spokes. Working together, these players can establish the company's core AI assets and capabilities, such as common analytics tools, data processes, and delivery methodologies. But as time passes and processes become standardized, these experts can reside within the spokes just as (or more) effectively.

Business model complexity. The greater the number of business functions, lines of business, or geographies AI tools will support, the greater the need to build guilds of AI experts (of, say, data scientists or designers). Companies with complex businesses often consolidate these guilds in the hub and then assign them out as needed to business units, functions, or geographies.

The pace and level of technical innovation required. When they need to innovate rapidly, some companies put more gray-area strategy and capability building in the hub so they can monitor industry and technology changes better and quickly deploy AI resources to head off competitive challenges.

Let's return to the two financial institutions we discussed earlier. Both faced competitive pressures that required rapid innovation. However, their analytics maturity and business complexity differed.

The institution that placed its analytics teams within its hub had a much more complex business model and relatively low AI maturity. Its existing AI expertise was primarily in risk management. By concentrating its data scientists, engineers, and many other gray-area experts within the hub, the company ensured that all business units and functions could rapidly access essential know-how when needed.

The second financial institution had a much simpler business model that involved specializing in fewer financial services. This bank also had substantial AI experience and expertise. So it was able to decentralize its AI talent, embedding many of its gray-area analytics, strategy, and technology experts within the business-unit spokes.

As these examples suggest, some art is involved in deciding where responsibilities should live. Every organization has distinctive capabilities and competitive pressures, and the three key factors must be considered in totality, rather than individually. For example, an organization might have high business complexity and need very rapid innovation (suggesting it should shift more responsibilities to the hub) but also have very mature AI capabilities (suggesting it should move them to the spokes). Its leaders would have to weigh the relative importance of all three factors to determine where, on balance, talent would most effectively be deployed. Talent levels (an element of AI maturity) often have an outsize influence on the decision. Does the organization have enough data experts that, if it moved them permanently to the spokes, it could still fill the needs of all business units, functions, and geographies? If not, it would probably be better to house them in the hub and share them throughout the organization.

Oversight and execution

While the distribution of AI and analytics responsibilities varies from one organization to the next, those that scale up AI have two things in common:

A governing coalition of business, IT, and analytics leaders. Fully integrating AI is a long journey. Creating a joint task force to oversee it will ensure that the three functions collaborate and share accountability, regardless of how roles and responsibilities are divided. This group, which is often convened by the chief analytics officer, can also be instrumental in building momentum for AI initiatives, especially early on.

Assignment-based execution teams. Organizations that scale up AI are twice as likely to set up interdisciplinary teams within the spokes. Such teams bring a diversity of perspectives together and solicit input from frontline staff as they build, deploy, and monitor new AI capabilities. The teams are usually assembled at the outset of each initiative and draw skills from both the hub and the spokes. Each generally includes the manager in charge of the new AI tool's success (the "product owner"), translators, data architects, engineers and scientists, designers, visualization specialists, and business analysts. These teams address implementation issues early and extract value faster.

For example, at the Asian Pacific retailer that was using AI to optimize store space and inventory placement, an interdisciplinary execution team helped break down walls between merchandisers (who determined how items would be displayed in stores) and buyers (who chose the range of products). Previously, each group had worked independently, with the buyers altering the AI recommendations as they saw fit. That led to a mismatch between inventory purchased and space available. By inviting both groups to collaborate on the further development of the AI tool, the team created a more effective model that provided a range of weighted options to the buyers, who could then choose the best ones with input from the merchandisers. At the end of the process, gross margins on each product category that had applied the tool increased by 4% to 7%.

Educating Everyone

To ensure the adoption of AI, companies need to educate everyone, from the top leaders down. To this end some are launching internal AI academies, which typically incorporate classroom work (online or in person), workshops, on-the-job training, and even site visits to experienced industry peers. Most academies initially hire external faculty to write the curricula and deliver training, but they also usually put in place processes to build in-house capabilities.

Every academy is different, but most offer four broad types of instruction:

Leadership
Most academies strive to give senior executives and business-unit leaders a high-level understanding of how AI works and ways to

10 Ways to Derail an AI Program

DESPITE BIG INVESTMENTS, many organizations get disappointing results from their AI and analytics efforts. What makes programs go off track? Companies set themselves up to fail when:

1. They lack a clear understanding of advanced analytics, staffing up with data scientists, engineers, and other key players without realizing how advanced and traditional analytics differ.

2. They don't assess feasibility, business value, and time horizons, and launch pilots without thinking through how to balance short-term wins in the first year with longer-term payoffs.

3. They have no strategy beyond a few use cases, tackling AI in an ad hoc way without considering the big-picture opportunities and threats AI presents in their industry.

4. They don't clearly define key roles, because they don't understand the tapestry of skill sets and tasks that a strong AI program requires.

5. They lack "translators," or experts who can bridge the business and analytics realms by identifying high-value use cases, communicating business needs to tech experts, and generating buy-in with business users.

6. They isolate analytics from the business, rigidly centralizing it or locking it in poorly coordinated silos, rather than organizing it in ways that allow analytics and business experts to work closely together.

7. They squander time and money on enterprisewide data cleaning instead of aligning data consolidation and cleanup with their most valuable use cases.

8. They fully build out analytics platforms before identifying business cases, setting up architectures like data lakes without knowing what they'll be needed for and often integrating platforms with legacy systems unnecessarily.

9. They neglect to quantify analytics' bottom-line impact, lacking a performance management framework with clear metrics for tracking each initiative.

10. They fail to focus on ethical, social, and regulatory implications, leaving themselves vulnerable to potential missteps when it comes to data acquisition and use, algorithmic bias, and other risks, and exposing themselves to social and legal consequences.

For more details, read "Ten Red Flags Signaling Your Analytics Program Will Fail" on McKinsey.com.

identify and prioritize AI opportunities. They also provide discussions of the impact on workers' roles, barriers to adoption, and talent development, and offer guidance on instilling the underlying cultural changes required.

Analytics

Here the focus is on constantly sharpening the hard and soft skills of data scientists, engineers, architects, and other employees who are responsible for data analytics, data governance, and building the AI solutions.

Translator

Analytics translators often come from the business staff and need fundamental technical training—for instance, in how to apply analytical approaches to business problems and develop AI use cases. Their instruction may include online tutorials, hands-on experience shadowing veteran translators, and a final "exam" in which they must successfully implement an AI initiative.

End user

Frontline workers may need only a general introduction to new AI tools, followed by on-the-job training and coaching in how to use them. Strategic decision makers, such as marketers and finance staff, may require higher-level training sessions that incorporate real business scenarios in which new tools improve decisions about, say, product launches.

Reinforcing the Change

Most AI transformations take 18 to 36 months to complete, with some taking as long as five years. To prevent them from losing momentum, leaders need to do four things:

Walk the talk

Role modeling is essential. For starters, leaders can demonstrate their commitment to AI by attending academy training.

But they also must actively encourage new ways of working. AI requires experimentation, and often early iterations don't work out as planned. When that happens, leaders should highlight what was learned from the pilots. That will help encourage appropriate risk taking.

The most effective role models we've seen are humble. They ask questions and reinforce the value of diverse perspectives. They regularly meet with staff to discuss the data, asking questions such as "How often are we right?" and "What data do we have to support today's decision?"

The CEO of one specialty retailer we know is a good example. At every meeting she goes to, she invites attendees to share their experience and opinions—and offers hers last. She also makes time to meet with business and analytics employees every few weeks to see what they've done—whether it's launching a new pilot or scaling up an existing one.

Make businesses accountable

It's not uncommon to see analytics staff made the owners of AI products. However, because analytics are simply a means of solving business problems, it's the business units that must lead projects and be responsible for their success. Ownership ought to be assigned to someone from the relevant business, who should map out roles and guide a project from start to finish. Sometimes organizations assign different owners at different points in the development life cycle (for instance, for proof of value, deployment, and scaling). That's a mistake too, because it can result in loose ends or missed opportunities.

A scorecard that captures project performance metrics for all stakeholders is an excellent way to align the goals of analytics and business teams. One airline company, for instance, used a shared scorecard to measure rate of adoption, speed to full capability, and business outcomes for an AI solution that optimized pricing and booking.

Track and facilitate adoption

Comparing the results of decisions made with and without AI can encourage employees to use it. For example, at one commodity company, traders learned that their non-AI-supported forecasts were typically right only half the time—no better than guessing. That discovery made them more open to AI tools for improved forecasting.

Teams that monitor implementation can correct course as needed. At one North American retailer, an AI project owner saw store managers struggling to incorporate a pilot's output into their tracking of store performance results. The AI's user interface was difficult to navigate, and the AI insights generated weren't integrated into the dashboards the managers relied on every day to make decisions. To fix the issue, the AI team simplified the interface and reconfigured the output so that the new data stream appeared in the dashboard.

Provide incentives for change

Acknowledgment inspires employees for the long haul. The CEO of the specialty retailer starts meetings by shining a spotlight on an employee (such as a product manager, a data scientist, or a frontline worker) who has helped make the company's AI program a success. At the large retail conglomerate, the CEO created new roles for top performers who participated in the AI transformation. For instance, he promoted the category manager who helped test the optimization solution during its pilot to lead its rollout across stores—visibly demonstrating the career impact that embracing AI could have.

Finally, firms have to check that employees' incentives are truly aligned with AI use. This was not the case at a brick-and-mortar retailer that had developed an AI model to optimize discount pricing so that it could clear out old stock. The model revealed that sometimes it was more profitable to dispose of old stock than to sell it at a discount, but the store personnel had incentives to sell everything, even at steep discounts. Because the AI recommendations contradicted their standard, rewarded practice, employees became suspicious of the tool and ignored it. Since their sales incentives were also closely tied to contracts and couldn't easily be changed, the organization ultimately updated the AI model to recognize the trade-off between profits and the incentives, which helped drive user adoption and lifted the bottom line.

The actions that promote scale in AI create a virtuous circle. The move from functional to interdisciplinary teams initially brings together the diverse skills and perspectives and the user input needed to build effective tools. In time, workers across the organization absorb new collaborative practices. As they work more closely with colleagues in other functions and geographies, employees begin to think bigger—they move from trying to solve discrete problems to completely reimagining business and operating models. The speed of innovation picks up as the rest of the organization begins to adopt the test-and-learn approaches that successfully propelled the pilots.

As AI tools spread throughout the organization, those closest to the action become increasingly able to make decisions once made by those above them, flattening organizational hierarchies. That encourages further collaboration and even bigger thinking.

The ways AI can be used to augment decision making keep expanding. New applications will create fundamental and sometimes difficult changes in workflows, roles, and culture, which leaders will need to shepherd their organizations through carefully. Companies that excel at implementing AI throughout the organization will find themselves at a great advantage in a world where humans and machines working together outperform either humans or machines working on their own.

Originally published in July–August 2019. Reprint R1904C

How Smart, Connected Products Are Transforming Companies

by Michael E. Porter and James E. Heppelmann

THE EVOLUTION OF PRODUCTS into intelligent, connected devices—which are increasingly embedded in broader systems—is radically reshaping companies and competition.

Smart thermostats control a growing array of home devices, transmitting data about their use back to manufacturers. Intelligent, networked industrial machines autonomously coordinate and optimize work. Cars stream data about their operation, location, and environment to their makers and receive software upgrades that enhance their performance or head off problems before they occur. Products continue to evolve long after entering service. The relationship a firm has with its products—and with its customers—is becoming continuous and open-ended.

In our previous HBR article, "How Smart, Connected Products Are Transforming Competition" (November 2014), we examined the implications external to the firm, looking in detail at how smart, connected products affect rivalry, industry structure, industry boundaries, and strategy. (See the sidebar "Implications for Strategy.") In this article we'll explore their internal implications: how the nature of smart, connected products substantially changes the work of

Implications for Strategy

IN A SMART, CONNECTED WORLD, COMPANIES face 10 new strategic decisions. A firm's choices will have a major impact on every activity in its value chain.

1. Which set of smart, connected product capabilities and features should the company pursue?

2. How much functionality should be embedded in the product and how much in the cloud?

3. Should the company pursue an open or closed system?

4. Should the company develop the full set of smart, connected product capabilities and infrastructure internally or outsource to vendors and partners?

5. What data must the company capture, secure, and analyze to maximize the value of its offering?

6. How does the company manage ownership and access rights to its product data?

7. Should the company fully or partially disintermediate distribution channels or service networks?

8. Should the company change its business model?

9. Should the company enter new businesses by monetizing its product data through selling it to outside parties?

10. Should the company expand its scope?

Source: "How Smart, Connected Products Are Transforming Competition," *Harvard Business Review*, November 2014

virtually every function within the manufacturing firm. The core functions—product development, IT, manufacturing, logistics, marketing, sales, and after-sale service—are being redefined, and the intensity of coordination among them is increasing. Entirely new functions are emerging, including those to manage the staggering quantities of data now available. All of this has major implications for the classic organizational structure of manufacturers. What is under way is perhaps the most substantial change in the manufacturing firm since the Second Industrial Revolution, more than a century ago.

Idea in Brief

A Radical Shift

Smart, connected products are forcing companies to redefine their industries and rethink nearly everything they do, beginning with their strategies. This article, the second in a two-part series, focuses on the impact of these products on companies' operations and organizational structure.

New Relationships

The unprecedented data and capabilities that smart, connected products provide are changing the way firms interact with their customers. Those relationships are becoming continuous and open-ended.

New Processes

The new product capabilities and infrastructure and the data they generate are reshaping the work of virtually every function in the value chain, including product development, IT, manufacturing, logistics, marketing, sales, and after-sale service. In addition, far more intense coordination among functions is now required.

New Structures

New forms of cross-functional collaboration and entirely new functions are emerging. These include unified data organizations, units to continuously improve products postsale, and groups charged with optimizing customer relationships.

The New Product Capabilities

To fully grasp how smart, connected products are changing how companies work, we must first understand their inherent components, technology, and capabilities—something that our previous article examined. To recap:

All smart, connected products, from home appliances to industrial equipment, share three core elements: *physical* components (such as mechanical and electrical parts); *smart* components (sensors, microprocessors, data storage, controls, software, an embedded operating system, and a digital user interface); and *connectivity* components (ports, antennae, protocols, and networks that enable communication between the product and the product cloud, which runs on remote servers and contains the product's external operating system).

Smart, connected products require a whole new supporting technology infrastructure. This "technology stack" provides a gateway

The new technology stack

Smart, connected products require companies to build and support an entirely new technology infrastructure. This "technology stack" is made up of multiple layers, including new product hardware, embedded software, connectivity, a product cloud consisting of software running on remote servers, a suite of security tools, a gateway for external information sources, and integration with enterprise business systems.

IDENTITY AND SECURITY
Tools that manage user authentication and system access, as well as secure the product, connectivity, and product cloud layers

EXTERNAL INFORMATION SOURCES
A gateway for information from external sources—such as weather, traffic, commodity and energy prices, social media, and geomapping—that informs product capabilities

INTEGRATION WITH BUSINESS SYSTEMS
Tools that integrate data from smart, connected products with core enterprise business systems such as ERP, CRM, and PLM

PRODUCT CLOUD

Smart product applications
Software applications running on remote servers that manage the monitoring, control, optimization, and autonomous operation of product functions

Rules/analytics engine
The rules, business logic, and big data analytical capabilities that populate the algorithms involved in product operation and reveal new product insights

Application platform
An application development and execution environment enabling the rapid creation of smart, connected business applications using data access, visualization, and run-time tools

Product data database
A big-data database system that enables aggregation, normalization, and management of real-time and historical product data

CONNECTIVITY

Network communication
The protocols that enable communications between the product and the cloud

PRODUCT

Product software
An embedded operating system, onboard software applications, an enhanced user interface, and product control components

Product hardware
Embedded sensors, processors, and a connectivity port/antenna that supplement traditional mechanical and electrical components

Source: "How Smart, Connected Products Are Transforming Competition," *Harvard Business Review*, November 2014

for data exchange between the product and the user and integrates data from business systems, external sources, and other related products. The technology stack also serves as the platform for data storage and analytics, runs applications, and safeguards access to products and the data flowing to and from them. (See the exhibit "The new technology stack.")

This infrastructure enables extraordinary new product capabilities. First, products can *monitor* and report on their own condition and environment, helping to generate previously unavailable insights into their performance and use. Second, complex product operations can be *controlled* by the users, through numerous remote-access options. That gives users the unprecedented ability to customize the function, performance, and interface of products and to operate them in hazardous or hard-to-reach environments.

Third, the combination of monitoring data and remote-control capability creates new opportunities for *optimization*. Algorithms can substantially improve product performance, utilization, and uptime, and how products work with related products in broader systems, such as smart buildings and smart farms. Fourth, the combination of monitoring data, remote control, and optimization algorithms allows *autonomy*. Products can learn, adapt to the environment and to user preferences, service themselves, and operate on their own.

Reshaping the Manufacturing Company

To create products and get them to customers, manufacturers perform a wide range of activities, which generally take place in a standard set of functional units: research and development (or engineering), IT, manufacturing, logistics, marketing, sales, after-sale service, human resources, procurement, and finance. The new capabilities of smart, connected products alter every activity in this value chain. At the core of what is reshaping the value chain is data.

The new data resource

Before products became smart and connected, data was generated primarily by internal operations and through transactions across the value chain—order processing, interactions with suppliers, sales interactions, customer service visits, and so on. Firms supplemented that data with information gathered from surveys, research, and other external sources. By combining the data, companies knew something about customers, demand, and costs—but much less about the functioning of products. The responsibility for defining and analyzing data tended to be decentralized within functions and siloed. Though functions shared data (sales data, for example, might be used to manage service parts inventory), they did so on a limited, episodic basis.

Now, for the first time, these traditional sources of data are being supplemented by another source—the product itself. Smart, connected products can generate real-time readings that are unprecedented in their variety and volume. Data now stands on par with people, technology, and capital as a core asset of the corporation and in many businesses is perhaps becoming the decisive asset.

This new product data is valuable by itself, yet its value increases exponentially when it is integrated with other data, such as service histories, inventory locations, commodity prices, and traffic patterns. In a farm setting, data from humidity sensors can be combined with weather forecasts to optimize irrigation equipment and reduce water use. In fleets of vehicles, information about the pending service needs of each car or truck, and its location, allows service departments to stage parts, schedule maintenance, and increase the efficiency of repairs. Data on warranty status becomes more valuable when combined with data on product use and performance. Knowing that a customer's heavy use of a product is likely to result in a premature failure covered under warranty, for example, can trigger preemptive service that may preclude later costly repairs.

Data analytics

As the ability to unlock the full value of data becomes a key source of competitive advantage, the management, governance, analysis, and security of that data is developing into a major new business function.

While individual sensor readings are valuable, companies often can unearth powerful insights by identifying patterns in thousands of readings from many products over time. For example, information from disparate individual sensors, such as a car's engine temperature, throttle position, and fuel consumption, can reveal how performance correlates with the car's engineering specifications. Linking combinations of readings to the occurrence of problems can be useful, and even when the root cause of a problem is hard to deduce, those patterns can be acted on. Data from sensors that measure heat and vibration, for example, can predict an impending bearing failure days or weeks in advance. Capturing such insights is the domain of big data analytics, which blend mathematics, computer science, and business analysis techniques.

Big data analytics employ a family of new techniques to understand those patterns. A challenge is that the data from smart, connected products and related internal and external data are often unstructured. They may be in an array of formats, such as sensor readings, locations, temperatures, and sales and warranty history. Conventional approaches to data aggregation and analysis, such as spreadsheets and database tables, are ill-suited to managing a wide variety of data formats. The emerging solution is a "data lake," a repository in which disparate data streams can be stored in their native formats. From there, the data can be studied with a set of new data analytics tools. Those tools fall into four categories: descriptive, diagnostic, predictive, and prescriptive. (For more details, see the exhibit "Creating new value with data.")

To better understand the rich data generated by smart, connected products, companies are also beginning to deploy a tool called a "digital twin." Originally conceived by the Defense Advanced Research Projects Agency (DARPA), a digital twin is a 3-D virtual-reality replica of a physical product. As data streams in, the twin evolves to reflect how the physical product has been altered and used and the environmental conditions to which it has been exposed. Like an avatar for the actual product, the digital twin allows the company to visualize the status and condition of a product that may be thousands of miles away. Digital twins may also provide new insights into how products can be better designed, manufactured, operated, and serviced.

Creating new value with data

Data from smart, connected products is generating insights that help businesses, customers, and partners optimize product performance. Simple analytics, applied by individual products to their own data, reveal basic insights; more-sophisticated analytics, applied to product data that has been pooled into a "lake" with data from external and enterprise sources, unearth deeper insights.

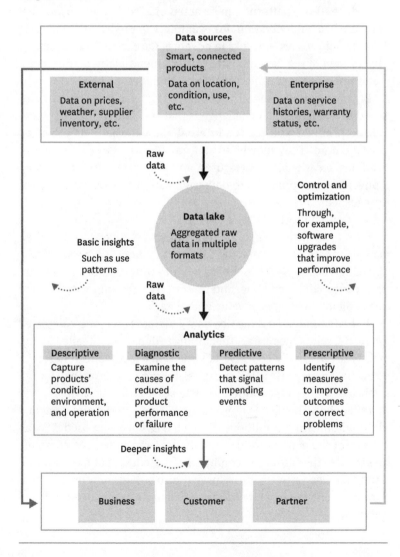

Data sources

Smart, connected products
Data on location, condition, use, etc.

External
Data on prices, weather, supplier inventory, etc.

Enterprise
Data on service histories, warranty status, etc.

Raw data

Data lake
Aggregated raw data in multiple formats

Control and optimization
Through, for example, software upgrades that improve performance

Basic insights
Such as use patterns

Raw data

Analytics

Descriptive	Diagnostic	Predictive	Prescriptive
Capture products' condition, environment, and operation	Examine the causes of reduced product performance or failure	Detect patterns that signal impending events	Identify measures to improve outcomes or correct problems

Deeper insights

Business   **Customer**   **Partner**

Transforming the Value Chain

The powerful new data available to companies, together with new configurations and capabilities of smart, connected products, is restructuring the traditional functions of business—sometimes radically. This transformation started with product development but is playing out across the value chain. As it spreads, functional boundaries are shifting, and new functions are being created.

Product development

Smart, connected products require a fundamental rethinking of design. At the most basic level, product development shifts from largely mechanical engineering to true interdisciplinary systems engineering. Products have become complex systems that contain software and may have as much or more software in the cloud. That's why design teams are shifting from a majority of mechanical engineers to a majority of software engineers, and some manufacturers, like GE, Airbus, and Danaher, are establishing offices in software-engineering hubs like Boston and Silicon Valley.

Smart, connected products also call for product design principles that depart dramatically from tradition:

Low-cost variability. In conventional products, variability is costly because it requires variation in physical parts. But the software in smart, connected products makes variability far cheaper. For example, John Deere used to manufacture multiple versions of engines, each providing a different level of horsepower. It now can alter the horsepower of a standard physical engine using software alone. Similarly, digital user interfaces can replace dials and buttons, making it easy and less expensive to modify a product by, say, changing control options. Meeting customer needs for variability through software, not hardware, is a critical new design discipline.

Manufacturing goes beyond production of the physical object, because operating a smart, connected product requires a supporting cloud-based system.

Variability is needed not only across customer segments but also across geographies. Software also makes it easier to localize products for different countries and languages. However, emerging local regulations for data standards, such as those governing the transmission of data across national boundaries, require duplication of data storage infrastructure or applications. Such regulations are introducing new country and regional differences, sometimes for political reasons.

Evergreen design. In the old model, products were designed in discrete generations. The new product incorporated a full set of desired improvements, and the design was then fixed until the next generation. Smart, connected products, however, can be continually upgraded via software, often remotely. Products also can be fine-tuned to meet new customer requirements or solve performance issues. The performance of ABB Robotics' industrial machines, for example, can be remotely monitored and adjusted by end users during operation. Companies can release new features that are works-in-process, not finalized. Recently, Tesla began putting an "autopilot" system in its cars, but with the intention of enhancing the system's capabilities over time through remote software updates.

New user interfaces and augmented reality. The digital user interface of a smart, connected product can be put into a tablet or smartphone application, enabling remote operation and even eliminating the need for controls in the product itself. As noted, these interfaces are less costly to implement and easier to modify than physical controls, and they enable greater operator mobility.

Some products have begun incorporating a powerful new interface technology called "augmented reality." Through a smartphone or tablet pointed at the product, or through smart glasses, augmented reality applications tap into the product cloud and generate a digital overlay of the product. This overlay contains monitoring, operating, and service information that makes supporting or servicing the product more efficient. Constructing these powerful digital interfaces is another critical new design discipline.

Ongoing quality management. Testing that tries to replicate the conditions in which customers will use products has long been part of product development. The aim is to ensure that new offerings will live up to their specifications and to minimize warranty claims. Smart, connected products take quality management several steps farther, enabling continuous monitoring of real-world performance data, allowing companies to identify and address design problems that testing failed to expose. In 2013, for example, batteries in two Tesla Model S cars were punctured and caught fire after drivers struck metal objects in the road. The road conditions and speeds leading to the punctures had not been simulated in testing, but Tesla was able to reconstruct them. The company then sent a software update to all vehicles that would raise their suspension under those conditions, significantly reducing the chances of further punctures.

Connected service. Product designs now need to incorporate additional instrumentation, data collection capability, and diagnostic software features that monitor product health and performance and warn service personnel of failures. And as software increases functionality, products can be designed to allow more remote service.

Support for new business models. Smart, connected products let companies switch from transactional selling to product-as-a-service models. However, this shift has product design implications. When a product is delivered as a service, the responsibility for and associated cost of maintenance remain with the manufacturer, and that can alter several design parameters. This is especially true when multiple customers share the product—as is the case at Smoove, a bike-sharing service in France. Smoove has designed its smart, connected bikes with chainless driveshafts, puncture-resistant tires, and antivandal nuts to improve durability and prevent theft.

Products delivered as services must also capture usage data so that customers are appropriately charged. This requires clear thinking about the type and location of sensors, what data will be gathered, and how often it should be analyzed. When Xerox evolved from selling copiers to charging by the document, it added sensors on the photoreceptor drum, feeder output tray, and toner cartridge to enable accurate billing and facilitate the sale of consumables like paper and toner.

System interoperability. As products become components of broader systems, the opportunities for design optimization multiply. Through codesign, companies can simultaneously develop and enhance hardware and software across a family of products, including those of other companies. Take Nest Labs' self-learning thermostat. It was designed with an application programming interface that allows it to exchange information with other products, such as Kevo's smart lock. When the home owner enters the house, the Kevo lock communicates that to the Nest thermostat, which then adjusts the temperature to the home owner's preference.

Manufacturing

Smart, connected products create new production requirements and opportunities. They may even shift final assembly to the customer site, where the last step is loading and configuring software. But more radical still, manufacturing now goes beyond the production of the physical object, because a functioning smart, connected product requires a cloud-based system for operating it throughout its life.

Smart factories. The new capabilities of smart, connected machines are reshaping the operations of manufacturing plants themselves, where machines increasingly can be linked together in systems. In new initiatives like Industrie 4.0 (in Germany) and Smart Manufacturing (in the United States), networked machines fully automate and optimize production. For example, a production machine can detect a potentially dangerous malfunction, shut down other equipment that could be damaged, and direct maintenance staff to the problem.

GE's Brilliant Factories initiative uses sensors (retrofitted on existing equipment or designed into new equipment) to stream information into a data lake, where it can be analyzed for insights on cutting

A New Era of Lean

SMART, CONNECTED PRODUCTS WILL HELP make people, materials, energy, and plant and equipment far more productive, and the repercussions for business processes will be felt throughout the economy.

We will see a whole new era of "lean." Data flowing to and from products will allow product use and activities across the value chain to be streamlined in countless new ways.

Waste will be cut or eliminated. Sensors in products can identify the need for service before a component fails, reducing downtime. Or they can reveal that maintenance isn't yet necessary. An oil change, for instance, will take place only after oil contamination has hit a certain threshold, rather than according to a schedule. New data analytics will lead to previously unattainable efficiency improvements.

Wasted capacity will be driven out. Because products will report on their location and use, we will be able to make the most of them. Smart, connected elevators, for example, can predict and act on user demand patterns, reducing wait times and electricity use. A building that once might have needed six elevators can provide better service with four. Product-as-a-service models will allow customers to pay only for what they actually need. With data and connectivity, the sharing of assets (think cars or bikes) will become possible or easier than ever before.

---

downtime and improving efficiency. In one plant, this approach doubled the production of defect-free units.

Simplified components. The physical complexity of products often diminishes as functionality moves from mechanical parts to software. This shift eliminates physical components, along with the production steps needed to build and assemble them. Withings, for example, has reduced its blood pressure monitor to a cuff and sensor, eliminating the display through an app that can track blood pressure and send updates directly to clinicians. Similarly, manufacturers of aircraft, automobiles, and boats are moving toward "glass cockpits," in which a single screen displays numerous configurable gauges. As the physical complexity of products decreases, however, the quantity of sensors and software rises, introducing new parts and complexity.

Reconfigured assembly processes. Manufacturing has evolved toward standardized platforms, with customization of individual products occurring later and later in the assembly process. This approach reaps economies of scale and lowers inventory. Smart, connected products go even further. Software in the product or in the cloud can be loaded or configured well after the product leaves the factory, by a field service technician or even by the customer. New apps can be added or touchscreen keyboards set up for different languages. Product design changes can be incorporated at the last minute, even after delivery.

Continuous product operations. Until now, manufacturing has been a discrete process that ended once the product was shipped. Smart, connected products, however, cannot operate without a cloud-based technology stack. In effect, the stack is a component of the product—one the manufacturer must operate and improve throughout the product's life. In this sense, manufacturing becomes a permanent process.

Logistics

The earliest roots of smart, connected products were in logistics, which involve the movement of production inputs and outputs and the delivery of products. Commercialized in the 1990s, radio frequency identification, or RFID, tags greatly enhanced the ability to track shipments. Indeed, the term "Internet of Things" was coined by a founder of MIT's Auto-ID Center, which specialized in RFID research. Today's smart, connected products take tracking to an entirely new level. Now it can be done continuously, wherever products are, without the need for a scanner, and provides rich information on not just their current location but also their location history, their condition (their temperature, say, or exposure to stresses), and their surrounding environment.

We believe that smart, connected products will ultimately move logistics to a whole new generation. For example, the management of large, far-flung fleets of vehicles is being transformed by the ability to remotely monitor each vehicle's position and function, check

its local traffic and weather conditions, and provide drivers with
an optimized delivery schedule. And automated drones capable of
dropping packages directly on the customer's doorstep—which are
now being tested by Amazon, Google, and DHL—could revolutionize
the delivery process for many products.

Marketing and sales

The ability to remain connected to the product and track how it's
being used shifts the focus of a company's customer relationship
from selling—often a predominantly one-time transaction—to maximizing the customer's value from the product over time. This opens
up important new requirements and opportunities for marketing
and sales.

New ways to segment and customize. The data from smart, connected products provides a much sharper picture of product use,
showing, for example, which features customers prefer or fail to use.
By comparing usage patterns, companies can do much finer customer segmentation—by industry, geography, organizational unit,
and even more-granular attributes. Marketers can apply this deeper
knowledge to tailor special offers or after-sale service packages, create features for certain segments, and develop more-sophisticated
pricing strategies that better match price and value at the segment
or even the individual customer level.

New customer relationships. As the focus shifts to providing
continual value to the customer, the product becomes a means of
delivering that value, rather than the end itself. And because a manufacturer remains connected to customers via the product, it has a
new basis for direct and ongoing dialogue with them. Companies are
beginning to see the product as a window into the needs and satisfaction of customers, rather than relying on customers to learn
about product needs and performance.

All Traffic Solutions, for example, makes smart, connected
road signs that measure traffic speed and volume. The signs allow
advanced data mining of traffic patterns and help law enforcement

and other customers remotely monitor and manage traffic flows. The company's relationship with customers has shifted from selling signs to selling long-term services that improve safety without the need for police intervention. The signs are simply devices through which traffic management services are customized and delivered.

New business models. Having full transparency about how customers use products helps companies develop entirely new business models. Take Rolls-Royce's pioneering "power-by-the-hour" model, in which airlines pay for the time jet engines are used in flight, rather than a fixed price plus charges for maintenance and repairs. Today many industrial companies are beginning to offer their products as services—a move that has major implications for sales and marketing. The goal of salespeople becomes customer success over time, instead of just making the sale. That involves creating "win-win" scenarios for the customer and the company.

A focus on systems, not discrete products. As products become components of larger systems, the customer value proposition broadens. Product quality and features need to be supplemented by interoperability with related products. Companies must decide where to play in this new world: Will they compete at the product level; by offering a family of closely linked products; by creating a platform that cuts across all related products; or by doing all three? Sales and marketing teams will need broader knowledge to position their offerings as components of larger smart, connected systems. Partnerships will often be necessary to fill product gaps or connect products to leading platforms. Salespeople will need to be trained to sell with those partners, and incentives will need to accommodate more-complex revenue-sharing models.

Consider SmartThings, which sells in the increasingly crowded do-it-yourself home-automation space. The company has positioned itself with both consumers and manufacturers as an easy-to-use platform for smart home devices. Its platform has a simple user interface and provides an array of standard sensors that measure such things as moisture, smoke, temperature, and motion.

The sensors, which can be attached to any home object, automate lighting, home security, and energy conservation. The company also makes it easy to connect smart home devices from a variety of other manufacturers to its hub and has built an extensive partner ecosystem that already encompasses more than 100 compatible products.

After-sale service

For manufacturers of long-lived products, such as industrial equipment, after-sale service can represent significant revenues and profits—partly because traditional service delivery is inherently inefficient. Technicians often must inspect a product to identify the reason for a failure and the parts needed to correct it and then make a second trip to perform the repair.

Smart, connected products improve service and efficiency and enable a fundamental shift from reactive service to preventive, proactive, and remote service:

One-stop service. Because technicians can diagnose problems remotely, they can have the parts needed for repairs in their trucks the first time they arrive at the customer site. They can also have supporting information for executing the repairs. Only one visit is necessary, and success rates rise.

Remote service. Smart, connected products make delivering service via connectivity increasingly feasible. In many cases products can be repaired by remote technicians in the same way that computers are now often fixed. The blood- and urine-analysis equipment made by Sysmex is a good example. Sysmex originally added connectivity to its instruments to allow remote monitoring but now uses it to provide service as well. Service technicians can access just as much information about a machine when they are off-site as when they are on-site. Often they can fix it by rebooting it, delivering a software upgrade, or talking an on-site medical technician through the process. As a result, service costs, equipment downtime, and customer satisfaction have improved dramatically.

Preventive service. Using predictive analytics, organizations can anticipate problems in smart, connected products and take action. Diebold, for example, monitors its automated teller machines for early signs of trouble. It performs the necessary maintenance remotely, if possible, or dispatches a technician to adjust or replace parts. The company can also update a machine with preventive fixes when feature enhancements are added, sometimes remotely.

Augmented-reality-supported service. The vast amounts of data that smart, connected products gather are creating new ways for service personnel to work individually, together, and with customers. One emerging approach utilizes the augmented reality overlays we described earlier. When these include information about a product's service needs and step-by-step repair instructions, service efficiency and effectiveness can increase dramatically.

New services. The data, connectivity, and analytics available through smart, connected products are expanding the traditional role of the service function and creating new offerings. Indeed, the service organization has become a major source of business innovation in manufacturing, driving increased revenue and profit through new value-added services such as extended warranties and comparative benchmarking across a customer's equipment, fleet, or industry. The array of solutions that Caterpillar has developed to help customers manage its construction and mining equipment is a good example. After gathering and analyzing data for each machine deployed at a work site, Caterpillar's service teams advise customers on where to locate equipment, when fewer machines could suffice, when to add new equipment to reduce bottlenecks, and how to achieve higher fuel efficiency throughout a fleet.

Security

Until recently, IT departments in manufacturing companies have been largely responsible for safeguarding firms' data centers, business systems, computers, and networks. With the advent of smart, connected devices, the game changes dramatically. The job of ensuring IT security now cuts across all functions.

Every smart, connected device may be a point of network access, a target of hackers, or a launchpad for cyberattacks. Smart, connected products are widely distributed, exposed, and hard to protect with physical measures. Because the products themselves often have limited processing power, they cannot support modern security hardware and software.

Smart, connected products share some familiar vulnerabilities with IT in general. For example, they are susceptible to the same type of denial-of-service attack that overwhelms servers and networks with a flood of access requests. However, these products have major new points of vulnerability, and the impact of intrusions can be more severe. Hackers can take control of a product or tap into the sensitive data that moves between it, the manufacturer, and the customer. On the TV program *60 Minutes,* DARPA demonstrated how a hacker could gain complete control of a car's acceleration and braking, for example. The risk posed by hackers penetrating aircraft, automobiles, medical equipment, generators, and other connected products could be far greater than the risks from a breach of a business e-mail server.

Customers expect products and their data to be safe. So a firm's ability to provide security is becoming a key source of value—and a potential differentiator. Customers with extraordinary security needs, such as the military and defense organizations, may demand special services.

Security will affect multiple functions. Clearly the IT function will continue to play a central role in identifying and implementing best practices for data and network security. And the need to embed security in product design is crucial. Risk models must consider threats across all potential points of access: the device, the network to which it is connected, and the product cloud. New risk-mitigation techniques are emerging: The U.S. Food and Drug Administration, for example, has mandated that layered authentication levels and timed usage sessions be built into all medical devices to minimize the risk to patients. Security can also be enhanced by giving customers or users the ability to control when data is transmitted to the cloud and what type of data the manufacturer can collect. Overall, knowledge and best practices for security in a smart, connected world are rapidly evolving.

Data privacy and the fair exchange of value for data are also increasingly important to customers. Creating data policies and communicating them to customers is becoming a central concern of legal, marketing, sales and service, and other departments. In addition to addressing customers' privacy concerns, data policies must reflect ever-stricter government regulations and transparently define the type of data collected and how it will be used internally and by third parties.

Human resources

A manufacturer of smart, connected products is a cross between a software company and a traditional product company. This mix demands new skills across the value chain, as well as new working styles and cultural norms.

New expertise. The skills needed to design, sell, and service smart, connected products are in high demand but short supply. Indeed, manufacturers are experiencing a growing sense of urgency about finding the right talent as their skill requirements shift from mechanical engineering to software engineering, from selling products to selling services, and from repairing products to managing product uptime.

Manufacturers will have to hire experts in applications engineering, user interface development, and systems integration, and, most notably, data scientists capable of building and running the automated analytics that help translate data into action. The business or data analyst of the past is evolving into a new type of professional, who must possess both technical and business acumen as well as the ability to communicate insights from analytics to business and IT leaders.

The shortage of these new skills is especially acute in traditional manufacturing centers, many of which are different from technology hubs. So some manufacturers are establishing a physical presence in hot spots such as Boston and Silicon Valley, which combine a presence in advanced manufacturing with academic centers, makers of B2B hardware and software, and emerging producers of smart, connected products. Schneider Electric, for example, is moving its U.S. headquarters to Boston. Over the next decade, manufacturers can accelerate their learning and improve recruiting by being in such clusters. But they will also need new recruiting models, like internship programs with local universities and liaison programs to "borrow" talent from leading technology vendors.

New cultures. Manufacturing smart, connected products requires far more coordination across functions and disciplines than traditional manufacturing does. It also involves integrating staff with varied work styles and from more-diverse backgrounds and cultures—which can be challenging. For instance, the "clock speed" of software development is generally much faster than that of traditional manufacturing. HR organizations will have to rethink many aspects of organizational structure, policies, and norms.

New compensation models. Manufacturers will also need new approaches to attracting and motivating talent. Perks like job flexibility, concierge services, sabbaticals, and free time to work on side projects of personal interest are the norm in high-tech firms employing the type of talent manufacturing companies will increasingly require.

Implications for Organizational Structure

The shifting nature of work throughout the value chain is ushering in a historic organizational transformation of the manufacturing firm. Jeff Immelt, the CEO of General Electric, once said that every industrial company must become a software company. This statement reflects the fact that software is becoming an essential part of products. Beyond this, software firms have already moved in directions essential to competing in smart, connected products, such as

Lessons from the Software Industry

online discussion (handwritten margin note)

MANY OF THE ORGANIZATIONAL SHIFTS that smart, connected products are bringing to manufacturing mirror changes that have already taken root in the software industry. This is not surprising, since the evolution to smart, connected products requires a traditional manufacturer to build what is essentially an internal software company.

The software industry, with an entirely digital product, was early to deploy its products both on premise and in the cloud and to support them remotely. Software companies also were in the forefront in improving products continuously, including after the sale.

The organizational lessons that other industries can draw from software fall into five categories:

1. **Shorter development cycles:** The software industry has moved away from periodic releases of major products to smaller, incremental releases of upgrades and enhancements. Because of this, companies can get new products to market more quickly and respond faster to customer needs. Agile product-development processes—which emphasize daily collaboration between developers and marketers, weekly delivery of enhancements, continual course corrections, and ongoing testing of customer satisfaction—are best practice in software development.

2. **Product-as-a-service business models:** Software is undergoing a sectorwide transition to service-oriented business models. Customers purchase software on a subscription basis, paying only for what they need when they need it, instead of buying "shelfware" that sits idle.

---

evergreen design, remote upgrading, and product-as-a-service models. (See the sidebar "Lessons from the Software Industry.")

Yet the transformation of the manufacturing firm will be even bigger than what software companies have undergone. While incorporating software, the cloud, and data analytics, manufacturing firms must continue to design, produce, and support complex physical products.

Which aspects of the organizational structure will be affected? As Jay W. Lorsch and Paul R. Lawrence argued in the classic work *Organization and Environment,* every organizational structure must combine two basic elements: differentiation and integration. Dissimilar

This turns the product into an operating, rather than capital, expense, and hugely simplifies deployment (which happens via the cloud). To support this new model, software companies have learned to carefully track customer usage and satisfaction.

3. **Focus on customer success:** The shift toward software-as-a-service models has led to the rise of customer success organizations inside software companies. Given the ease with which customers can change vendors, ensuring that they receive superior ongoing value from products is critical. Many software companies now have customer engagement teams dedicated to pursuing that goal.

4. **Products as part of broader systems:** Most software is deployed as part of a larger "stack" of business tools, whose value is enhanced by their integration. Successful software companies often provide application program interfaces and other tools that enable easy integration of their product with third-party software. In addition, software companies often encourage the formation of developer communities to create new uses for their products.

5. **Analytics as a competitive advantage:** Software companies, especially those in e-commerce, have long understood the power of data analytics in generating customer value. Companies with an advertising revenue model use analytics to serve up ads at the right time—when customers are most likely to notice and act on them. Increasingly, software companies are also mining data on use to identify bugs with the highest impact on customers.

---

tasks, such as sales and engineering, need to be "differentiated," or organized into distinct units. At the same time, the activities of those separate units need to be "integrated" to coordinate and align them. Smart, connected products have a major impact on both differentiation and integration in manufacturing.

In the classic structure, a manufacturing business is divided into functional units, such as R&D, manufacturing, logistics, sales, marketing, after-sale service, finance, and IT. (While there is also a geographic dimension of organizational structure, which adds a layer of complexity, it is less affected by smart, connected products per se.) These functional units enjoy substantial autonomy. Though integration across them is essential, much of it tends to be relatively episodic and tactical. In addition to achieving alignment on the overall strategy and business plan, functions need to coordinate to manage key handoffs in the product life cycle (design to manufacturing, sales to service, and so on) and capture feedback from the field that will improve processes and products (information on defects, customer reactions). Integration across functional units happens largely through the business unit leadership team and through the design of formal processes for product development, supply chain management, order processing, and the like, in which multiple units have roles.

With the emergence of smart, connected products, however, this classic model breaks down. The need to coordinate across product design, cloud operation, service improvement, and customer engagement is continuous and never ends, even after the sale. Periodic handoffs no longer suffice. Intense, ongoing coordination becomes necessary across multiple functions, including design, operations, sales, service, and IT. Functional roles overlap and blur. In addition, completely new and critical functions emerge—for instance, to manage all the new data and the new open-ended customer relationships. At the broadest level, the rich data and real-time feedback from smart, connected products challenge the traditional centralized command-and-control model of management in favor of distributed but highly integrated choices and continuous improvement.

On top of this, manufacturers must keep producing and supporting conventional products, and that's not likely to change—in some cases, for decades. Even in today's progressive, established manufacturing companies, smart, connected products represent less than half of all products sold. The continued coexistence of the new and the old will complicate organizational structures.

What will the new manufacturing organization look like? Organizational structures are in rapid flux, even among the leading makers of smart, connected products. However, a number of important shifts are becoming evident. The first is more and deeper collaboration and integration between IT and R&D. Over time those

A new organizational structure

Smart, connected products require functions within manufacturing firms to collaborate in new ways. As a result, firms' structures are rapidly evolving. A new functional unit focused on data management is starting to appear. Though rare, units focused on ongoing product development and customer success are also beginning to be recognized.

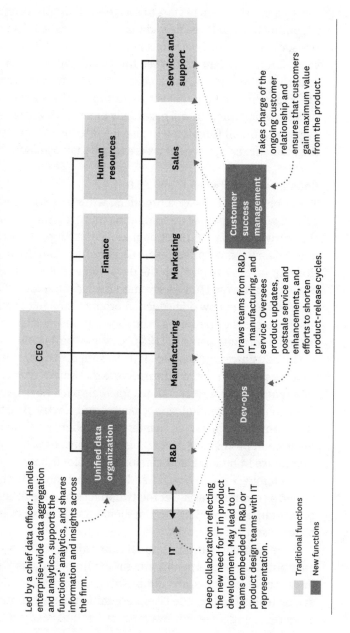

Led by a chief data officer. Handles enterprise-wide data aggregation and analytics, supports the functions' analytics, and shares information and insights across the firm.

Deep collaboration reflecting the new need for IT in product development. May lead to IT teams embedded in R&D or product design teams with IT representation.

Draws teams from R&D, IT, manufacturing, and service. Oversees product updates, postsale service and enhancements, and efforts to shorten product-release cycles.

Takes charge of the ongoing customer relationship and ensures that customers gain maximum value from the product.

CEO

Unified data organization

IT

R&D

Manufacturing

Finance

Human resources

Marketing

Sales

Service and support

Dev-ops

Customer success management

Traditional functions

New functions

units—and others—may start to merge. In addition, companies are beginning to form three new kinds of units: unified data organizations, development-operations groups (or dev-ops), and customer success management units. (See the exhibit "A new organizational structure.") Meanwhile, product and data security activities are rapidly expanding and now cut across multiple units, though it remains unclear what structure will eventually emerge. Ultimately, virtually every traditional function will also need to be restructured, given the dramatic realignment of tasks and roles taking place.

Collaboration between IT and R&D

Traditionally, R&D created products, while IT was primarily concerned with companywide computing infrastructure and managing the software tools the functional groups used, such as computer-aided design, enterprise resource planning, and customer relationship management. With the development of smart, connected products, however, IT must assume a more central role. IT hardware and software are now embedded in products and in the entire technology stack. The question is, who should be responsible for this new technology infrastructure: IT, R&D, or some combination of both?

Only IT currently has the skills to support the software-based technologies and related infrastructure that smart, connected products require. R&D organizations, for their part, have been good at developing and combining mechanical and electrical components, and many have begun to master the challenge of incorporating software in products. Few R&D organizations, however, have deep experience in building and managing the cloud-based elements of the technology stack. Now, IT and R&D must integrate their activities on a continual basis. Yet the two functions have little history of collaboration on product development—and in some organizations have a history of animosity.

Various organizational models for this new relationship are emerging. Some companies are embedding IT teams within R&D departments. Others are establishing cross-functional product design teams that include IT representation while maintaining separate reporting lines. For example, at Ventana Medical Systems, a maker of smart, connected lab equipment, the IT and R&D teams now work jointly on product development, with IT weighing in heavily on choices about what product functionality should be delivered in the cloud and when software updates are needed. At Thermo Fisher Scientific, a scientific instrument leader, members of the IT department work directly inside R&D, with a dotted-line reporting structure and shared goals. This has improved Thermo Fisher's effectiveness at defining and building the product cloud; securely capturing, analyzing, and storing product data; and distributing data both internally and to customers.

A unified data organization
Because of the growing volume, complexity, and strategic importance of data, it is no longer desirable or even feasible for each function to manage data by itself, build its own data analytics capability, or handle its own data security. To get the most out of the new data resources, many companies are creating dedicated data groups that consolidate data collection, aggregation, and analytics, and are responsible for making data and insights available across functions and business units. The research firm Gartner predicts that by 2017 as many as a quarter of all large firms will have dedicated data units.

The new data organizations usually are led by a C-level executive, the chief data officer, who reports to the CEO or sometimes to the CFO or CIO. He or she is responsible for unified data management, educating the organization on how to apply data resources, overseeing data rights and access, and driving the application of advanced data analytics across the value chain. Ford Motor Company, for example, recently appointed a chief data and analytics officer to develop and execute an enterprise-wide vision for data analysis. The CDO is spearheading the company's use of smart, connected product data to understand customer preferences, shape future strategies for connected cars, and restructure internal processes.

Dev-ops
The imperatives of evergreen product design, continuous product operation and support, and ongoing product upgrades are creating

a need for a new functional group, sometimes called dev-ops. (The term comes from the software industry, where it is used to describe a collaborative, cross-functional software development and deployment method.) The dev-ops unit is responsible for managing and optimizing the ongoing performance of connected products after they have left the factory. It brings together software-engineering experts from the traditional product-development organization (the "dev") with staff members from IT, manufacturing, and service who are responsible for product operation (the "ops").

Dev-ops organizes and leads teams that shorten product-release cycles, manage product updates and patches, and deliver new services and enhancements postsale. It oversees the frequent release of small, carefully tested batches of product changes into the shared cloud, ideally with no disruption to existing products and users in the field. The dev-ops organization also leads the work to enhance preventive service models and product maintenance.

Customer success management
A third new organizational unit, which also has an analogue in the software industry, is responsible for managing the customer experience and ensuring that customers get the most from the product. This task is crucial with smart, connected products, especially to ensure renewals in product-as-a-service models. The customer success management unit does not necessarily replace sales or service units but assumes primary responsibility for customer relationships after the sale. This unit performs roles that traditional sales and service organizations are not equipped for and don't have incentives to adopt: monitoring product use and performance data to gauge the value customers capture and identifying ways to increase it. This new unit does not operate as a self-contained silo but collaborates on an ongoing basis with marketing, sales, and service.

Customer success units are changing the management of customer relationships. Historically, customer surveys and call centers have been the principal ways companies gather insights about product use and determine when a customer relationship is in jeopardy.

Companies typically hear most from customers when something goes wrong—and often not until it is too late.

With smart, connected products, the product itself becomes a sensor that gauges the value customers are receiving. Through the data it generates, a product can tell companies a lot about the customer experience: about product use and performance, customer preferences, and customer satisfaction. Such insights can prevent customer defections and reveal where a customer could benefit from additional product capabilities or services.

Shared responsibility for security

In most companies, executive oversight of security is in flux. Security may report to the chief information officer, the chief technology officer, the chief data officer, or the chief compliance officer. Whatever the leadership structure, security cuts across product development, dev-ops, IT, the field service group, and other units. Especially strong collaboration among R&D, IT, and the data organization is essential. The data organization, along with IT, will normally be responsible for securing product data, defining user access and rights protocols, and identifying and complying with regulations. The R&D and dev-ops teams will take the lead on reducing vulnerabilities in the physical product. IT and R&D will often be jointly responsible for maintaining and protecting the product cloud and its connections to the product. However, the organizational model for managing security is still being written.

Making the Transition

How do we get from here to there? The organizational changes we have described are substantial. Today centralized data groups are just beginning to appear, and the integration of IT and R&D is in a very early stage. Dev-ops and customer success management units are rare, but their roles are starting to be recognized and differentiated. Over time these may emerge as formal functional units.

At manufacturers in fields like aircraft, medical devices, and agricultural equipment, smart, connected products will need to coexist with traditional products for a sustained period. This means that the organizational transformation we are describing will be evolutionary, not revolutionary, and old and new structures will often need to operate in parallel.

Given the scope of the changes, and the scarcity of skills and experience in smart, connected products, many companies will need to pursue hybrid or transitional structures. This will allow scarce talent to be leveraged, experience pooled, and duplication avoided.

What could this transitional structure look like? At the business unit level many companies have encouraged organic smart, connected product initiatives. A function like IT might be assigned the lead role for smart, connected product strategy and deployment. Or a special steering committee made up of the functional heads may be asked to champion and oversee this effort. Some firms are acquiring or partnering with focused software companies for smart, connected product initiatives, injecting new talent and perspectives into their organizations. Caterpillar recently made such a move by investing in Uptake, a predictive analytics firm.

At the corporate level in multibusiness companies, overlay structures are being put in place to evangelize the smart, connected products opportunity, identify the best places to start, avoid duplication, build a critical mass of talent and expertise, and oversee technology infrastructure. These units often have CEO or senior management sponsorship. We are seeing three models emerging:

Stand-alone business unit

A separate new unit, with profit-and-loss responsibility, is put in charge of supporting the company's smart, connected products strategy. The unit aggregates the talent and mobilizes the technology and assets needed to bring such new offerings to market, working with all affected business units. The Bosch Group is one company that has formed such a dedicated unit, Bosch Software Innovations. It enables the company's product-based business units and external customers to build services for smart, connected products.

A new stand-alone unit is free from the constraints of legacy business processes and organizational structures. In some companies, as expertise, infrastructure, and experience grow, leadership may start shifting back to the business units over time. In other cases, stand-alone units may deter, rather than enable, initiatives in the individual business units. Also, knowledge acquired by a stand-alone unit may disseminate more slowly across the firm.

Center of excellence

In this model, a separate corporate unit houses key expertise on smart, connected products. It does not have profit-and-loss responsibility but is a cost center that business units can tap. GE has such a center of excellence in Silicon Valley.

Cross-business-unit steering committee

This approach involves convening a committee of thought leaders across the various business units, who champion opportunities, share expertise, and facilitate collaboration. Such committees usually lack formal decision-making authority, which can limit their ability to drive change.

The Broader Implications

Smart, connected products are dramatically changing opportunities for value creation in the economy. A revolution is under way in manufacturing. The effects are not confined to manufacturing, however, but are spreading to other industries that use—or could use—smart, connected products, including services. (See the sidebar "How Smart, Connected Products Change Services.") And the impact of smart, connected products is still in the early innings.

Smart, connected products reshape not only competition, as we detailed in our previous article, but the very nature of the manufacturing firm, its work, and how it is organized. They are creating the first true discontinuity in the organization of manufacturing firms in modern business history. Many of the same organizational changes and challenges will spread to other fields as well.

For companies grappling with the transition, organizational issues are now center stage—and there is no playbook. We are just

How Smart, Connected Products Change Services

WHILE THE EFFECTS OF SMART, connected products begin in manufacturing, they flow to service industries as well.

Many service industries, including airlines, hospitality, health care, and financial services, rely on products that will become smart and connected. An airline with smart, connected planes, onboard flight systems, and baggage compartments can operate with far greater efficiency. Maintenance issues, for example, can be identified in flight, and the needed parts and expertise can be waiting when the plane lands. A laundromat at a college dormitory with smart, connected washers and dryers can inform users about machine availability and when loads are done. The washers and dryers can instantly notify maintenance personnel of failures, enabling rapid repair.

In health care, the utilization of expensive equipment, space, and clinical staff will be substantially improved, producing better care and patient experiences. Smart medical devices (like smart, connected pacemakers) can allow clinicians to track patients remotely and take more-appropriate and timely action. The opportunities for such monitoring—and for integrating disparate real-time data to gain new insights and inform lifestyle improvements—are game changing.

Even low-tech services will incorporate smart, connected devices. A cleaning company will place sensors in washroom doors or meeting rooms in order to focus on just the spaces that need cleaning. A parking garage will install sensors in individual parking spaces. A smartphone app will guide drivers to open spaces, reducing congestion and improving space utilization. The app will also enable ticketless, barrier-free payment while allowing dynamic pricing that reflects minute-by-minute demand patterns.

And entirely new services will be created. Uber has disrupted traditional taxi and livery businesses through its ability to tap huge unused transportation capacity. It's bringing many new drivers into the workforce and then identifying and matching the locations of drivers and passengers. The range of potential new services enabled by smart, connected products is limited only by the imagination.

beginning the process of rewriting the organization chart that has been in place for decades.

While the transition may be unsettling and destabilizing for many companies and raise real competitive challenges and security concerns, it is important to see smart, connected products first and foremost as a chance to improve economies and society. Because of these new products, we are poised to make great progress in environmental stewardship—substantially increasing the efficiency of land, water, and materials use, as well as energy efficiency and the productivity of the food system. They can help us achieve major advances in the human condition—in health, safety, mobility, training, and more—and help us with daily challenges, like easily finding a parking place.

And they position us to change the trajectory of society's overall consumption. After decades of ever more, ever cheaper, and ever more disposable everything, businesses and consumers may well need fewer things. Smart, connected products will free us to purchase only the goods and services we need, to share products that we do not use much, and to get more out of the products that we already have. Instead of tossing out old products for the next generation, we will hold on to products that are continually improved, upgraded, and modernized.

But what about work? Any major technological discontinuity raises inevitable concerns about its effect on jobs and opportunity, particularly in this day and age. We believe that the exponential opportunities for innovation presented by smart, connected products, together with the huge expansion of data they create about almost everything, will be a net generator of economic growth. These new types of products will not reduce our needs or the number of people required to meet them. Instead, new industries, new services, and new roles will be created that can allow more people to meet their aspirations.

What about those without the education and skills needed for the first wave of jobs in the transition? Those skills are in short supply, but the broader impact on employment and growth is likely to be positive. There will be more innovation and many new businesses.

And smart, connected products can be a leveler, allowing people to work more productively and in less rote and repetitive ways. Equip a service technician with an augmented reality application and a smartphone, and he or she can do a complex repair even with limited training. Less skilled workers can be coached and guided far more easily by experts. Imagine how a landscaper's job could change when yards and gardens are instrumented with sensors that provide information about the soil, watering history, plant health, and problem areas.

Manufacturers are leading the charge toward this future. The product and organizational transformations required are difficult and uncertain. The companies and other institutions that can speed this journey will prosper and make a profound difference for society.

The authors would like to acknowledge the extensive and invaluable assistance of Kathleen Mitford, Eric Snow, Alexandra Houghtalin, and Danny Bressler in the preparation of this article.

Originally published in October 2015. Reprint R1510G

The Age of Continuous Connection

by Nicolaj Siggelkow and Christian Terwiesch

A SEISMIC SHIFT IS UNDER WAY. Thanks to new technologies that enable frequent, low-friction, customized digital interactions, companies today are building much deeper ties with customers than ever before. Instead of waiting for customers to come to them, firms are addressing customers' needs the moment they arise—and sometimes even earlier. It's a win-win: Through what we call *connected strategies*, customers get a dramatically improved experience, and companies boost operational efficiencies and lower costs.

Consider the MagicBands that Disney World issues all its guests. These small wristbands, which incorporate radio-frequency-identification technology, allow visitors to enter the park, get priority access to rides, pay for food and merchandise, and unlock their hotel rooms. But the bands also help Disney locate guests anywhere in the park and then create customized experiences for them. Actors playing Disney characters, for example, can personally greet guests passing by ("Hey, Sophia! Happy seventh birthday!"). Disney can encourage people to visit attractions with idle capacity ("Short lines at Space Mountain right now!"). Cameras on various rides can automatically take photographs of guests, which Disney can use to create personalized memory books for them, without their ever having to pose for a picture.

Similarly, instead of just selling textbooks, McGraw-Hill Education now offers customized learning experiences. As students use the company's electronic texts to read and do assignments, digital technologies track their progress and feed data to their teachers and to the company. If someone is struggling with an assignment, her teacher will find out right away, and McGraw-Hill will direct the student to a chapter or video offering helpful explanations. Nike, too, has gotten into the game. It can now connect with customers daily, through a wellness system that includes chips embedded in shoes, software that analyzes workouts, and a social network that provides advice and support. That new model has allowed the company to transform itself from a maker of athletic gear into a purveyor of health, fitness, and coaching services.

It's easy to see how Disney, McGraw-Hill, and Nike have used approaches like these to stay ahead of the competition. Many other companies are taking steps to develop their own connected strategies by investing substantially in data gathering and analytics. That's great, but a lot of them are now awash in so much data that they're overwhelmed and struggling to cope. How can managers think clearly and systematically about what to do next? What are the best ways to use all this new information to better connect with customers?

In our research we've identified four effective connected strategies, each of which moves beyond traditional modes of customer interaction and represents a fundamentally new business model. We call them *respond to desire, curated offering, coach behavior,* and *automatic execution.* What's innovative here is not the technologies these strategies incorporate but the ways that companies deploy those technologies to develop continuous relationships with customers.

Below, we'll define these new connected strategies and explore how you can make the most of the ones you choose to adopt. But first let's take stock of the old model they're leaving behind.

Buy What We Have

Most companies still interact with customers only episodically, after customers identify their needs and seek out products or services to meet them. You might call this model *buy what we have.* In it

Idea in Brief

The Old Approach

Companies used to interact with customers only episodically, when customers came to them.

The New Approach

Today, thanks to new technologies, companies can address customers' needs the moment they arise—and sometimes even earlier. With connected strategies, firms can build deeper ties with customers and dramatically improve their experiences.

The Upshot

Companies need to make continuous connection a fundamental part of their business models. They can do so with four strategies: respond to desire, curated offering, coach behavior, and automatic execution.

companies work hard to provide high-quality offerings at a competitive price and base their marketing and operations on the assumption that they'll engage only fleetingly with their customers.

Here's a typical buy-what-we-have experience: One Tuesday, working from home, David is halfway through printing a batch of urgent letters when his toner cartridge runs out. It's maddening. He *really* doesn't have time for this. Grumbling, he hunts around for his keys, gets into his car, and drives 15 minutes to the nearest office supply store. There he wanders the aisles looking for the toner section, which turns out to be an entire wall of identical-looking cartridges. After scanning the options and hoping that he recalls his printer model correctly, he finds the cartridge he needs, but only in a multipack, which is expensive. He sets off in search of a staff member who might know if the store has any single cartridges, and eventually he locates a manager, who disappears into the back of the store to check.

Much time passes. When the manager at last returns, it's to report regretfully that the store is sold out of single cartridges. Because he has to get his letters done, David decides to buy the multipack. He grabs one and heads to the checkout counter to pay, only to find himself waiting in a long line. When he finally gets home, an hour or two later, he's not a happy guy.

We find it helpful to break the traditional customer journey into three distinct stages: *recognize,* when the customer becomes aware of a need; *request,* when he or she identifies a product or service that would satisfy this need and turns to a company to meet it; and *respond,* when the customer experiences how the company delivers the product or service. At each of these stages, David suffered a lot of discomfort, but at no point along the way did the toner company have any way of learning about his discomfort or alleviating it. Company and customer were poorly connected throughout, and both parties suffered.

It doesn't have to play out that way. Each of our four connected strategies could have helped improve David's customer experience at one or more of the stages and helped the company strengthen its business.

Let's explore specifically what each strategy entails.

Respond to Desire

This strategy involves providing customers with services and products they've requested—and doing so as quickly and seamlessly as possible. The essential capabilities here are operational: fast delivery, minimal friction, flexibility, and precise execution. Customers who enjoy being in the driver's seat tend to like this strategy.

To provide a good respond-to-desire experience, companies need to listen carefully to what customers want and make the buying process easy. In many cases, what matters most to customers is the amount of energy they have to expend—the less, the better!

That's certainly what David wanted in his search for a toner cartridge. So let's imagine a respond-to-desire strategy that might serve him well in the future.

Say that upon realizing that he needs a replacement, David goes online to his favorite retailer, types in his printer model, and with just a click or two makes a same-day order for the correct cartridge. His credit card number and address are already stored in the system, so the whole process takes just a minute or two. A few hours later his doorbell rings, and he has exactly what he needs.

Speed is critical in a lot of respond-to-desire situations. Users of Lyft and Uber want cars to arrive promptly. Health care patients want the ability to connect at any time of day or night with their providers. Retail customers want the products they order online to arrive as quickly as possible—a desire that Amazon has famously focused on satisfying, in the process redefining how it interacts with customers. Years ago it set up a "one click" process for ordering and payment, and more recently it has gone even further than that. Today you can give Alexa a command to order a particular product, and she'll take care of the rest of the customer journey for you. That's responding to desire.

Curated Offering

With this strategy, companies get actively involved in helping customers at an earlier stage of the customer journey: after the customers have figured out what they need but before they've decided how to fill that need. Executed properly, a curated-offering strategy not only delights customers but also generates efficiency benefits for companies, by steering customers toward products and services that firms can easily provide at the time. The key capability here is a personalized recommendation process. Customers who value advice—but still want to make the final decision—like this approach.

How might a curated-offering strategy serve David? Consider this scenario: He goes online to order his toner cartridge, and the site automatically suggests the correct one on the basis of what he has bought before. That spares him the hassle of finding the model number of his printer and figuring out which cartridge he needs. So now he just orders what the site suggests, and a few hours later, when his doorbell rings, he's had his needs smoothly and easily met.

Blue Apron and similar meal-kit providers have very effectively adopted the curated-offering strategy. This differentiates them from Instacart and many of the other grocery delivery services that have emerged in recent years, all of which are guided by a "you order, we deliver" principle—in other words, a respond-to-desire strategy. The Instacart approach might suit you better than spending time in a supermarket checkout line, but it doesn't relieve you of the burden of hunting for recipes and creating shopping lists of ingredients. Nor does it prevent you from overbuying when you do your shopping. Blue Apron helps on all those fronts, by presenting you with personally tailored offerings, creating an experience that many people find is more convenient, fun, and healthful than what they would choose on their own.

Coach Behavior

Both of the previous two strategies require customers to identify their needs in a timely manner, which (being human) we're not always good at. Coach-behavior strategies help with this challenge, by proactively reminding customers of their needs and encouraging them to take steps to achieve their goals.

Coaching behavior works best with customers who know they need nudging. Some people want to get in shape but can't stick to a workout regimen. Others need to take medications but are forgetful. In these situations a company can watch over customers and help them. Knowledge of a customer's needs might come from information that the person has previously shared with the firm or from observing the behavior of many customers. The essential capabilities involved are a deep understanding of customer needs ("What does the customer really want to achieve?") and the ability to gather and interpret rich contextual data ("What has the customer done or not done up to this point? Can she now enact behaviors that will get her closer to her goal?").

Here's what a coach-behavior strategy for David might look like: Perhaps the printer itself tracks the number of pages it has generated since David last changed the toner and sends that information back to the manufacturer, which knows that he will soon need a new cartridge. So it might email him a reminder to reorder. At the same time, it might encourage him to run the cleaning function on his printer—a suggestion that will help him avoid later inconveniences. Coached in this way, David will have his new printer cartridge before the old one runs out; he'll lose almost no time in replacing it; and he'll have a clean printer that performs at its best.

To implement coach-behavior approaches well, a company needs to receive information constantly from its customers so that it doesn't miss the right moment to suggest action. The technical challenge in this sort of relationship lies in enabling cheap and reliable two-way communication with customers. Traditionally, this had been difficult, but it's getting easier all the time. The advent of wearable devices, for example, allows health care companies to hover digitally over customers around the clock, constantly monitoring how they're doing.

Nike's new business model incorporates coach-behavior strategies. By making its customers part of virtual running clubs and tracking their runs, the company knows when it's time for their next workout, and through its app it can offer them audio training guides and plans. This kind of timely and personal connection builds trust and encourages customers to think of Nike as a health-and-fitness coach rather than just a shoe manufacturer, which in turn means that when the company's app nudges them to run, they're more likely to do it. This serves customers well, because it keeps them motivated and in shape. And it serves Nike well, of course, because customers who run more buy more shoes.

Automatic Execution

All the strategies we've discussed so far require customer involvement. But this last strategy allows companies to meet the needs of customers even before they've become aware of those needs.

In an automatic-execution strategy, customers authorize a company to take care of something, and from that point on the company handles everything. The essential elements here are strong trust, a rich flow of information from the customers, and the ability to use it to flawlessly anticipate what they want. The customers most open to automatic execution are comfortable having data stream constantly from their devices to companies they buy from and have faith that those companies will use their data to fulfill their needs at a reasonable price and without compromising their privacy.

Here's how automatic execution might work for David. When he buys his printer, he authorizes the manufacturer to remotely monitor his ink level and send him new toner cartridges whenever it gets low. From then on, the onus is on the company to manage his needs, and David is spared several hassles: recognizing that he's low on toner, figuring out how to get more, and buying it. Instead, he just goes about his business. When the time is right, his doorbell will ring, and he'll have exactly what he needs.

The growing internet of things is making all sorts of automatic execution possible. David's printer cartridge scenario isn't just hypothetical: Both HP and Brother already have programs that ship replacement toner to customers whenever their printers send out a "low ink" signal. Soon our refrigerators, sensing that we're almost out of milk, will be able to order more for delivery by tomorrow morning—but naturally only after checking our calendar to make sure we're not going on a vacation and wouldn't need milk after all.

Automatic execution will make people's lives easier and in some cases will even save lives. Consider fall-detection sensors, the small medical devices worn by many seniors. Initially, the companies who made them did so using the respond-to-desire model. If an elderly person who was wearing one fell and needed help, she could press a button that activated a distress call. That was good, but it didn't work if someone was too incapacitated to press the button. Now, though, internet-connected wearable technologies allow health care companies to monitor patients constantly in real time, which means people don't need to actively request assistance if and when they're in distress. Imagine a bracelet that monitors vital signs and uses an accelerometer to detect falls. If a person wearing the bracelet slips, tumbles down the basement stairs, and is knocked unconscious, the bracelet's sensor will immediately detect the emergency and summon help. That's automatic execution.

We're excited about automatic execution, but we want to stress that we don't see it as the best solution to all problems—or for all customers. People differ in the degree to which they feel comfortable sharing data and in having the companies serving them act on that data. One family might be delighted to receive an automatically

Which connected strategies should you use?

Connected strategy	Description	Key capability	Works best when	Works best for
Respond to desire	Customer expresses what she wants and when	Fast and efficient response to orders	Customers are knowledgeable	Customers who don't want to share too much data and who like to be in control
Curated offering	Firm offers tailored menu of options to customer	Making good personalized recommendations	The uncurated set of options is large and potentially overwhelming	Customers who don't mind sharing some data but want a final say
Coach behavior	Firm nudges customer to act to obtain a goal	Understanding customer needs and ability to gather and interpret rich data	Inertia and biases keep customers from achieving what's best for them	Customers who don't mind sharing personal data and getting suggestions
Automatic execution	Firm fills customer's need without being asked	Monitoring customers and translating incoming data into action	Customer behavior is very predictable and costs of mistakes are small	Customers who don't mind sharing personal data and having firms make decisions for them

generated personal memory book after a visit to Disney World, but another might think it's creepy and invasive. If companies want customers to make a lot of personal data available on an automated and continuous basis, they will need to prove themselves worthy of their customers' trust. They'll need to show customers that they'll safeguard the privacy and security of personal information and that they'll only recommend products and services in good faith. Breaking a customer's trust at this level could mean losing that customer—and possibly many other customers—forever.

A final important point: Given that companies are likely to have customers with different preferences, most firms will have to create a portfolio of connected strategies, which will require them to build a whole new set of capabilities. (See the table "Which connected strategies should you use?") One-size-fits-all usually won't work.

Repeat

Earlier, we mentioned that we like to think of the individual customer journey as having three stages: *recognize, request,* and *respond.* But there's actually a fourth stage—*repeat*—which is fundamental to any connected strategy, because it transforms stand-alone experiences into long-lasting, valuable relationships. It is in this stage that companies learn from existing interactions and shape future ones—and discover how to create a sustainable competitive advantage.

The repeat dimension of a connected strategy helps companies with two forms of learning.

First, it allows a company to get better at matching the needs of an individual customer with the company's existing products and services. Over time and through multiple interactions, Disney sees that a customer seems to like ice cream more than fries, and theater performances more than fast rides—information that then allows the company to create a more enjoyable itinerary for him. McGraw-Hill sees that a student struggles with compound-interest calculations, which lets it direct her attention to material that covers exactly that weakness. Netflix sees that a customer likes political satire, which allows it to make pertinent movie suggestions to her.

Second, in the repeat stage companies can learn at the population level, which helps them make smart adjustments to their portfolios of products and services. If Disney sees that the general demand for frozen yogurt is rising, it can increase the number of stands in its parks that serve frozen yogurt. If McGraw-Hill sees that many students are struggling with compound-interest calculations, it can refine its online module on that topic. If Netflix observes that many viewers like political dramas, it can license or produce new series in that genre.

Both of these loops have positive feedback effects. The better the company understands a customer, the more it can customize its offerings to her. The more delighted she is by this, the more likely she is to return to the company again, thus providing it with even more data. The more data the company has, the better it can customize its offerings. Likewise, the more new customers a company attracts through its superior customization, the better its population-level data is. The better its population data, the more it can create desirable products. The more desirable its products, the more it can attract new customers. And so on. Both learning loops build on themselves, allowing companies to keep expanding their competitive advantage.

Over time these two loops have another very important effect: They allow companies to address more-fundamental customer needs and desires. McGraw-Hill might find out that a customer wants not just to understand financial accounting but also to have a career on Wall Street. Nike might find out that a particular runner is interested not just in keeping fit but also in training to run a first marathon. That knowledge offers opportunities for companies to create an even wider range of services and to develop trusted relationships with customers that become very hard for competitors to disrupt.

We can't tell you where all this is headed, of course. But here's what we know: The age of "buy what we have" is over. If you want to achieve sustainable competitive advantage in the years ahead, connected strategies need to be a fundamental part of your business. This holds true whether you're a start-up trying to break into an existing industry or an incumbent firm trying to defend your market, and whether you deal directly with consumers or operate in a business-to-business setting. The time to think about connected strategies is now, before others in your industry beat you to it.

Originally published in May–June 2019. Reprint R1903C

The Problem with Legacy Ecosystems

by Maxwell Wessel, Aaron Levie, and Robert Siegel

AS AUTOMATION AND DIGITIZATION transform the economy, well-resourced incumbents in industry after industry are losing out to upstarts. Traditional retailers that have entered the e-commerce space appear no match for digital-native Amazon. Electric-vehicle sales at the world's most storied automotive companies consistently trail Tesla's. And even after substantial investments in technology, no taxicab consortium has been able to fend off Uber's attack.

Why is it that so few of the powerhouses of the 20th century are leaders in the new data-driven world?

The three of us have been exploring that question in a course called "The Industrialist's Dilemma" that we teach at Stanford University's Graduate School of Business. Part of the answer has already been suggested by Clayton Christensen and other business scholars. All companies' internal systems—their metrics, resource allocation processes, incentives, approaches to recruitment and promotion, and investment strategies—are set up to support their existing business models. These systems are generally well established and extremely difficult to change, and they often conflict with the needs of digital business models.

But the CEOs we interview in the classroom pinpoint a different challenge—one that arises because of how value is created in a digitized economy. Many of the most successful business models of the 21st century are built on being able to reach into peoples' lives, using software that generates information on customer habits and patterns of usage. These digital relationships provide a new level of intimacy, allowing firms to personalize their offerings and better orchestrate how they serve customers.

Most older companies, however, struggle to take advantage of the opportunity to extend their relationships with customers, because they're constrained by their existing value chains. A network of partners with fixed ways of doing business presents an *external* challenge, even if the *internal* challenges that go along with business model reinvention can be overcome.

Firms that have had relatively stable relationships with suppliers, competitors, collaborators, and customers for many years can't easily shake up those networks. But doing so may be essential for long-term survival. To better understand why, let's take a deeper look at ways in which the digital era has changed how we create and capture value.

Software Transforms Customer Relationships

Uber's success is not a story about big data. It's a story about small data obtained directly from customers in a new way. Uber realized that it didn't need to amass and analyze vast amounts of information about taxi usage; it simply had to capture the most meaningful piece of information about users at exactly the right time: *where* a potential rider is located *when* he or she needs a ride. And the company knew it could learn that if it had access to the customer's cell phone. Afforded such access, Uber could make a rider's experience easier and more convenient than taxicabs did.

Many of today's most iconic companies share a similar story: Their success is built on an ability to reach further into a customer's world than competitors do (or than anyone could have 20 years ago). The clearest examples are in the realm of connected devices. Tesla equips its cars with sensors and software to understand how customers drive and to offer them autopilot functions. Nest sells "smart" thermostats, smoke detectors, and video cameras that keep tabs on what's happening in users' homes in order to improve

Idea in Brief

The Question

Why do so many well-resourced, historically strong companies fail to keep pace with digital-native challengers?

The Answer

The failure stems partly from how hard it is to walk away from a successful business model. But there's another, subtler reason: The new disrupters know more about customers, because they have access to better data.

Recommendations

To build effective new business models that take advantage of digital technology, older companies need to agree on the way forward, adopt new performance metrics, and rebuild their supplier, distributor, and partner networks.

---

energy efficiency and safety. General Electric is reaching into its customers' industrial sites to monitor assets in real time, providing service alerts and changing maintenance schedules according to data gleaned from embedded software.

But it is not just connected products that enable companies to extend their relationships with customers. Consider Netflix: By instrumenting its apps to detect everything from where customers are geographically to when viewers stop watching a movie, the company is able to understand people's preferences intimately. The streaming-media giant uses this knowledge to provide timely recommendations and to source—or even create—content that people will love.

23andMe, a provider of genetic testing, also takes customer relations to a new level. Instead of simply sending test results to doctors and hospitals, as most labs do, 23andMe maintains a connection with clients, periodically sending them questionnaires, creating a community through online forums, and pointing people to relevant information about their health and genetics. Such ongoing engagement allows 23andMe to conduct innovative research while spending far less than competitors and continually gaining insights to share with clients.

The ability to connect more personally with customers creates immense opportunity for companies to capture data about the market, supply new products and services, and build extremely defensible network effects and feedback loops. But transforming a customer relationship is not simple; it often requires doing things differently up and down the value chain.

Disrupting Partnerships

Most corporate strategists fail to grasp that software alone won't transform their business model. Each of the aforementioned companies leverages software in innovative ways, but each also changed how products are distributed and serviced—and even how input materials are sourced.

Let's return to the example of Nest. Cofounder Tony Fadell told our class that an early differentiator for the company was that it chose to market its first product, the Learning Thermostat, directly to homeowners for do-it-yourself setup, bypassing the typical distribution and installation channel—professional contractors. Why does that matter? Nest's team knew that only a small fraction of thermostats were ever programmed to adjust a dwelling's temperature depending on the time of day, the day of the week, and the season—the process was just too complicated. To deliver on the promise of a thermostat that would actually program itself, Nest had to enable the device to learn the customer's temperature preferences and schedule. And for the software to work best, the team needed to create user profiles, ensure that the thermostat was connected to a home's wireless network, and confirm that the customer had the Nest mobile app on his or her phone.

Approaching product sales and installation differently made this possible. Without contractors in the supply chain, Nest could develop a user-friendly product from which customers could easily derive value. The company's decision to abandon the traditional distribution channel committed the team to building a strong retail strategy and a consumer-facing brand. But it disadvantaged professional installers and challenged the existing ecosystem.

As the case of Nest shows, when companies use digital technologies to form new relationships with customers, software development is only part of the process. Sometimes this is because companies seek to change customers' behavior at various points in the customer journey. Sometimes it is because delivering value involves using the data collected to supplant former partners. In either situation, business models and channel strategies must change in unison—requiring tough decisions that can upset long-standing partners.

The Need for Interdependence

In some circumstances, the shift from an industrial to a digital setting has even more radical consequences for partnerships than what we saw in the Nest example.

To understand why, we need to take a brief detour, to look at what scholars understand about how transformative innovations emerge and evolve. Clayton Christensen, drawing on the work of Alfred Chandler and other business historians, has observed that the need to restructure the extended value chain is common when major innovations are introduced—not just because business models are often in flux, but also because innovative product designs are still emerging. Early in the life of a new product, the inventors don't have a deep understanding of how to optimize different components of an innovation relative to one another. The first automobile manufacturers, for example, needed to maintain tight control over research, design, and manufacturing. Changes to one part of the car often meant changes throughout the automobile. For that reason, product development required an *interdependent* network of partners.

Over time, as more standard design architectures emerged, companies developed a sophisticated understanding of how the different components worked together—how transmissions relate to batteries, for instance, and how batteries relate to electrical systems. Components and subsystems could then be *modularized*. Today traditional automobile manufacturers have the luxury of allowing innovation to occur at the subsystem level; next-generation products will plug in easily to most car platforms. Such broad scope for

What's Different About Today's Information Technology?

FAR MORE BORN-DIGITAL COMPANIES REPLACE incumbents now than was the case a generation ago. That's because the nature of IT innovation has changed in fundamental ways.

In the 1990s most IT inventions (and investments) were designed to support large organizations' internal processes. Businesses like SAP, Oracle, and IBM were all about helping corporations operate more efficiently. At the time, infrastructure and applications were expensive and inflexible. It was easier to focus on automating processes than on disrupting how client businesses made their money. For those reasons, the first generation of IT benefited large organizations more often than not (although the displacement of employees caused some pain).

Today incredible improvements in the price and flexibility of IT infrastructure have aided newcomers across industries, enabling them to use technology to create businesses with operating models entirely different from those of their 20th-century peers. Further, the spread of the internet into our homes and onto our mobile devices has made it easier for digital innovators to reach customers directly. These innovators seek to *displace* rather than *support* legacy organizations—making it critical that older businesses pay close attention to what's changing and adapt when necessary.

---

independent partner activity is typical of mature technologies and mature industries.

However, the more dramatic the innovation, the more interdependence may be required. As we find our way into a world of autonomous and electric vehicles, a level of interdependence that resembles vertical integration seems needed again. Tesla's cars maintain some of the most interdependent architectures on the market. The automaker controls every component of its vehicles, including the hardware, the software that manages the complex electrical system, and the algorithms and sensors that enable the self-driving functions. And the tight control extends even further: Tesla owns its distribution channel, service network, and charging network. This integrated model allows the company to address all the challenges involved in producing autonomous and long-distance electric vehicles, along with fast-charging batteries. (There's a drawback, though—the model also creates operational complexity that might slow the company's expansion.)

Building a New Ecosystem

Let's assume we accept the first two points in this discussion—that advances in computing and communication allow businesses to extend their relationships with customers, and that taking advantage of these digital technologies requires companies to create a more interdependent architecture for the innovation. Then the implications become clear: Companies of all varieties will need to reshape their value chains. And sometimes this change will impact longtime partners in unfavorable ways.

Netflix, as we mentioned earlier, monitors everything its customers do and uses that information to power decisions ranging from content recommendations to content sourcing. But to do this effectively, it needed new ecosystem partners with compatible goals: content owners looking for "long tail syndication" (like the BBC), distribution vendors (like Amazon Web Services), and platform partners that would enable the instrumentation of applications (like Apple and Google).

Sometimes existing partners are eager to reinvent themselves. Sometimes they can be financially motivated to adapt to a company's new needs. But just as often, they have business models that are too difficult to change. Waiting hopefully for partners to catch up can jeopardize the long-term viability of a business. There's no easy way to manage the transition from one business model to another, but over the past year, we have observed a handful of best practices among the companies most successfully navigating this environment.

Establish what you *must* do

We've heard again and again from senior leaders about the importance of understanding what is needed to deliver value to their customers over the long run.

Why You Can't Afford to Fall Behind

SOME MANAGERS ACKNOWLEDGE THE VALUE of digital opportunities, but they want to know which attempts will succeed before they invest in projects that might upset existing operations or irritate channel partners. Unfortunately, taking a "wait and see" approach can be disastrous, because businesses that make data a core asset can build early and insurmountable leads. Those first-mover advantages exist because data has three beneficial characteristics:

Data Is Scalable

In the 20th century, delivering value to customers across the globe was difficult. Consider the hurdles Procter & Gamble faced in selling soap. Developing sufficient production capacity cost huge amounts. Setting up a global distribution network required mastery of complex operations. And hiring, training, and supervising a geographically diverse network of employees was enormously difficult. Today those processes are easier, but production is not infinitely scalable, distribution networks still need to be built, and managing a global workforce remains a challenge.

For digital businesses, however, offerings scale easily and cheaply. With some minor investments in language localization, software can extend immediately to any corner of the globe. Once an initial investment has been made in harvesting data and building the software system, it's possible to service customers anywhere at no incremental cost. That scalability alone is a game changer.

Reasonable people may argue about what the world will look like in the near term—or even the medium term. Fortunately, most rational executives *can* agree on the macro trends that will affect their industries over an extended period. By extrapolating from those trends, it's possible to come up with a thesis about how customers will consume products in the future. Deciding on the company's next steps may not be easy, but agreeing on the long-term predictions for the industry, the role the company can play under those scenarios, and the likely role of your partners is the way to begin making the necessary changes to take advantage of digital.

Consider one of the most prominent examples of digital transformation: General Electric. In 2008, when the company's senior executives met to discuss their long-term vision for the company, they all

Data Is Defensible

In an era of industrial production, it was often possible to learn your competitor's secrets. If a business had a proprietary production process, for example, a competitor could hire away a senior engineer. Data-intensive businesses, however, are inherently easier to defend. In the case of General Electric, for example, the company's maintenance software leverages trillions of data points to make predictions about future performance. No single person could possibly memorize the data or the rules that govern the system. Although someone might be able to replicate the prediction algorithm, without the petabytes of training data it would be impossible to deliver the same value to customers.

Data Is Reinforceable

For a company such as Netflix, which has been monitoring the likes and dislikes of customers for years, it's easy to build a basic recommendations algorithm. But Netflix's algorithm would not be impressive if it had stopped at iteration number one. Instead the company continually monitors what movies it recommends within categories and how people react. It uses the new information generated—whether a prediction was right or wrong—to augment and update the software. Over time, with each prediction, Netflix is able to grow its data set and deliver ever-greater value to customers. Many information-enriched services share this characteristic of constantly improving with incremental use.

agreed that industrial machines would soon be affected by the internet. They also agreed that once industrial assets were connected, the software could easily become the most differentiated part of a machine's offering, in much the same way that it had with personal computers. The timeline was open to question, but focusing on this inevitable change in industrial operations gave GE a polestar. It allowed the company to clearly outline expectations for employees and partners, and even to guide customers. For instance, the expectation that a singular data platform would be necessary to unify a company's industrial assets pointed GE to a future where it would provide software directly to customers instead of relying on system integrators to deliver it in a piecemeal fashion. Such clarity about what lay ahead also prompted company executives to continually question whether the decisions they were making were in the organization's long-term interest.

As business leaders everywhere start to deal with the pressures that digital change can bring, establishing some type of polestar is invaluable. If you know the direction in which you must move, it's much easier to decide when it's critical to disrupt your partners' legacy ways of doing business.

Develop better metrics

For many of the world's most successful businesses, the gauges of success have been in place for decades. Often these metrics—whether they're directed at internal employees or at external partners—focus on profitability or top-line revenue. Such output-based metrics are wonderful for mature businesses but less relevant in situations of digital innovation. A key factor in managing digital transformation is changing performance metrics to better highlight the failures of status quo operations and to support risk taking and experimentation.

Consider Ford Motor Company. When Mark Fields, Ford's CEO, joined one of our recent class sessions, students repeatedly asked about the risks automotive manufacturers face with autonomous vehicles. Fields acknowledged that the topic is a big one at Ford. Executives want to be ready to embrace new service and distribution paradigms that driverless cars might enable (paradigms that might upset a network of legacy partners). To that end, Ford has moved away from assessing executive performance largely on the basis of units sold annually; the company now also factors in the miles that are driven in Ford vehicles. Whether the company sells more new cars (the traditional measure of business performance) or increases the life span of existing vehicles (a metric that benefits few in the ecosystem beyond car owners), Ford executives will still be delivering toward their goals.

When the metrics change significantly, they can highlight and reinforce behavior that supports a company's digital strategy. As an example, Kaiser Permanente now pays less attention to common metrics such as hospital and doctor utilization within its network; instead it's focusing on maximizing "healthy life years" for patients. The emphasis on this new metric is helping the organization prioritize partnerships with wellness and technology companies over the hiring and optimal deployment of medical personnel.

Create commercial opportunities for partners

It's not possible to avoid adversely affecting some of your ecosystem partners. HBO might have to go around a cable company's set-top box and deliver apps directly to consumers. Chanel might have to build digital storefronts that threaten generations-old retail partners. General Electric or Siemens might offer software that competes directly with products from IBM, Accenture, and PTC. But as Patrick Collison, the CEO of the payments company Stripe, pointed out to our students, digital is not a zero-sum game. Stripe has been successful at partnering with existing financial institutions across the industry. Why? Because by decreasing the friction associated with building digital payment solutions, Stripe can help drive far more transaction volume through its partner institutions even while claiming its own small share of the market.

Where possible, it's vital for firms to create new opportunities for both themselves and their partners. As the overall economic pie gets bigger, firms can offer more—albeit smaller—pieces to others in the value chain. So while Accenture or A.T. Kearney might lose some systems integration revenue as GE starts delivering more standard software, GE makes a point of suggesting how everyone can benefit economically from this new way of doing business. For example, GE Digital's CTO, Harel Kodesh, regularly speaks with stakeholders about what the company is focused on and where it hopes partners like Accenture and A.T. Kearney can create applications.

Similarly, Kaiser Permanente is putting incentives in place to drive innovation in telemedicine. Visa is offering fraud-detection algorithms to affiliated developers. Whatever your business, creating commercial opportunity for your partners is a powerful tool in helping them embrace your vision.

———————

Establishing a polestar, changing performance metrics, and creating opportunities for partners can make it easier for industrial-era companies to manage the change to new, digital-enabled business models. But we don't mean to suggest that these transformations will be straightforward or pain-free. Companies will have to make difficult decisions that leave members of their legacy ecosystems behind. Some partners will necessarily turn into competitors. Others may simply become obsolete. But if business leaders can acknowledge that digital requires changes beyond software—and often beyond the direct control of their business—the opportunities are enormous.

Originally published in November 2016. Reprint R1611D

Your Workforce Is More Adaptable Than You Think

by Joseph B. Fuller, Judith K. Wallenstein, Manjari Raman, and Alice de Chalendar

MANY MANAGERS HAVE LITTLE FAITH in their employees' ability to survive the twists and turns of a rapidly evolving economy. "The majority of people in disappearing jobs do not realize what is coming," the head of strategy at a top German bank recently told us. "My call center workers are neither able nor willing to change."

This kind of thinking is common, but it's wrong, as we learned after surveying thousands of employees around the world. In 2018, in an attempt to understand the various forces shaping the nature of work, Harvard Business School's Project on Managing the Future of Work and the Boston Consulting Group's Henderson Institute came together to conduct a survey spanning 11 countries—Brazil, China, France, Germany, India, Indonesia, Japan, Spain, Sweden, the United Kingdom, and the United States—gathering responses from 1,000 workers in each. In it we focused solely on the people most vulnerable to changing dynamics: lower-income and middle-skills workers. The majority of them were earning less than the average household income in their countries, and all of them had no more than two years of postsecondary education. In each of eight countries—Brazil, China, France, Germany, India, Japan, the

United Kingdom, and the United States—we then surveyed at least 800 business leaders (whose companies differed from those of the workers we surveyed). In total we gathered responses from 11,000 workers and 6,500 business leaders.

What we learned was fascinating: The two groups perceived the future in significantly different ways. Given the complexity of the changes that companies are confronting today and the speed with which they need to make decisions, this gap in perceptions has serious and far-reaching consequences for managers and employees alike.

Predictably, business leaders feel anxious as they struggle to marshal and mobilize the workforce of tomorrow. In a climate of perpetual disruption, how can they find and hire employees who have the skills their companies need? And what should they do with people whose skills have become obsolete? The CEO of one multinational company told us he was so tormented by that last question that he had to seek counsel from his priest.

The workers, however, didn't share that sense of anxiety. Instead, they focused more on the opportunities and benefits that the future holds for them, and they revealed themselves to be much more eager to embrace change and learn new skills than their employers gave them credit for.

The Nature of the Gap

When executives today consider the forces that are changing how work is done, they tend to think mostly about disruptive *technologies*. But that's too narrow a focus. A remarkably broad set of forces is transforming the nature of work, and companies need to take them all into account.

In our research we've identified 17 forces of disruption, which we group into six basic categories. (See the sidebar "The Forces Shaping the Future of Work.") Our surveys explored the attitudes that business leaders and workers had toward each of them. In their responses, we were able to discern three notable differences in the ways that the two groups think about the future of work.

Idea in Brief

The Problem

As they try to build a workforce in a climate of perpetual disruption, business leaders worry that their employees can't—or just won't—adapt to the big changes that lie ahead. How can companies find people with the skills they will need?

What the Research Shows

Harvard Business School and the BCG Henderson Institute surveyed thousands of business leaders and workers around the world and discovered an important gap in perceptions: Workers are far more willing and able to embrace change than their employers assume.

The Solution

This gap represents an opportunity. Companies need to start thinking of their employees as a reserve of talent and energy that can be tapped by providing smart on-the-job skills training and career development.

The first is that *workers seem to recognize more clearly than leaders do that their organizations are contending with multiple forces of disruption, each of which will affect how companies work differently.* When asked to rate the impact that each of the 17 forces would have on their work lives, using a 100-point scale, the employees rated the force with the strongest impact 15 points higher than the force with the weakest impact. In comparison, there was only a nine-point spread between the forces rated the strongest and the weakest by managers.

In fact, the leaders seemed unable or unwilling to think in differentiated ways about the forces' potential for disruption. When asked about each force, roughly a third of them described it as having a significant impact on their organization today; close to half projected that it would have a significant impact in the future; and about a fifth claimed it would have no impact at all. That's a troubling level of uniformity, and it suggests that most leaders haven't yet figured out which forces of change they should make a priority.

Interestingly, workers appeared to be more aware of the opportunities and challenges of several of the forces. Notably, workers focused on the growing importance of the gig economy, and they ranked "freelancing and labor-sharing platforms" as the third most

The Forces Shaping the Future of Work

Accelerating Technological Change

- New technologies that replace human labor, threatening employment (such as driverless trucks)
- New technologies that augment or supplement human labor (for example, robots in health care)
- Sudden technology-based shifts in customer needs that result in new business models, new ways of working, or faster product innovation
- Technology-enabled opportunities to monetize free services (such as Amazon web services) or underutilized assets (such as personal consumption data)

Growing Demand for Skills

- General increase in the skills, technical knowledge, and formal education required to perform work
- Growing shortage of workers with the skills for rapidly evolving jobs

Changing Employee Expectations

- Increased popularity of flexible, self-directed forms of work that allow better work-life balance
- More widespread desire for work with a purpose and opportunities to influence the way it is delivered (for example, greater team autonomy)

---

significant of all 17 forces. Business leaders, however, ranked that force as the least significant.

The second difference that emerged from our survey was this: *Workers seem to be more adaptive and optimistic about the future than their leaders recognize.*

The conventional wisdom, of course, is that workers fear that technology will make their jobs obsolete. But our survey revealed that to be a misconception. A majority of the workers felt that advances such as automation and artificial intelligence would have a positive impact on their future. In fact, they felt that way about

Shifting Labor Demographics

- Need to increase workforce participation of underrepresented populations (such as elderly workers, women, immigrants, and rural workers)

Transitioning Work Models

- Rise of remote work
- Growth of contingent forms of work (such as on-call workers, temp workers, and contractors)
- Freelancing and labor-sharing platforms that provide access to talent
- Delivery of work through complex partner ecosystems (involving multiple industries, geographies, and organizations of different sizes), rather than within a single organization

Evolving Business Environment

- New regulation aimed at controlling technology use (for example, "robot taxes")
- Regulatory changes that affect wage levels, either directly (such as minimum wages or Social Security entitlements) or indirectly (such as more public income assistance or universal basic income)
- Regulatory shifts affecting cross-border flow of goods, services, and capital
- Greater economic and political volatility as members of society feel left behind

two-thirds of the forces. What concerned them most were the forces that might allow *other workers*—temporary, freelance, outsourced—to take their jobs.

When asked why they had a positive outlook, workers most commonly cited two reasons: the prospect of better wages and the prospect of more interesting and meaningful jobs. Both automation and technology, they felt, heralded opportunity on those fronts—by contributing to the emergence of more-flexible and self-directed forms of work, by creating alternative ways to earn income, and by making it possible to avoid tasks that were "dirty, dangerous, or dull."

In every country workers described themselves as more willing to prepare for the workplace of the future than managers believed them to be (in Japan, though, the percentages were nearly equal). Yet when asked what was holding workers back, managers chose answers that blamed employees, rather than themselves. Their most common response was that workers feared significant change. The idea that workers might lack the support they needed from employers was only their fifth-most-popular response.

That brings us to our third finding: *Workers are seeking more support and guidance to prepare themselves for future employment than management is providing.*

In every country except France and Japan, significant majorities of workers reported that they—and not their government or their employer—were responsible for equipping themselves to meet the needs of a rapidly evolving workplace. That held true across age groups and for both men and women. But workers also felt that they had serious obstacles to overcome: a lack of knowledge about their options; a lack of time to prepare for the future; high training costs; the impact that taking time off for training would have on wages; and, in particular, insufficient support from their employers. All are barriers that management can and should help workers get past.

What Employers Can Do to Help

The gap in perspectives is a problem because it leads managers to underestimate employees' ambitions and underinvest in their skills. But it also shows that there's a vast reserve of talent and energy companies can tap into to ready themselves for the future: their workers.

The challenge is figuring out how best to do that. We've identified five important ways to get started.

1. Don't just set up training programs—create a learning culture
If companies today engage in training, they tend to do it at specific times (when onboarding new hires, for example), to prepare

workers for particular jobs (like selling and servicing certain products), or when adopting new technologies. That worked well in an era when the pace of technological change was relatively slow. But advances are happening so quickly and with such complexity today that companies need to shift to a continuous-learning model—one that repeatedly enhances employees' skills and makes formal training broadly available. Firms also need to expand their portfolio of tactics beyond online and off-line courses to include learning on the job through project staffing and team rotations. Such an approach can help companies rethink traditional entry-level barriers (among them, educational credentials) and draw from a wider talent pool.

Consider what happens at Expeditors, a *Fortune* 500 company that provides global logistics and freight-forwarding services in more than 100 countries. In vetting job candidates, Expeditors has long relied on a "hire for attitude, train for skill" approach. Educational degrees are appreciated but not seen as critical for success in most roles. Instead, for all positions, from the lowest level right up to the C-suite, the company focuses on temperament and cultural fit. Once on staff, employees join an intensive program in which every member of the organization, no matter how junior or senior, undertakes 52 hours of incremental learning a year. This practice supports the company's promote-from-within culture. Expeditors' efforts seem to be working: Turnover is low (which means substantial savings in hiring, training, and onboarding costs); retention is high (a third of the company's 17,000 employees have worked at the company for 10 years or more); most senior leaders in the company have risen through the ranks; and several current vice presidents and senior vice presidents, along with the current and former CEOs, got their jobs despite having no college degree.

2. Engage employees in the transition instead of herding them through it

As companies transform themselves, they often find it a challenge to attract and retain the type of talent they need. To succeed, they have to offer employees pathways to professional and personal improvement—and must engage them in the process of change, rather than merely inform them that change is coming.

That's what ING Netherlands did in 2014, when it decided to reinvent itself. The bank's goal was ambitious: to turn itself into an agile institution almost overnight. The company's current CEO, Vincent van den Boogert, recalls that the company's leaders began by explaining the *why* and the *what* of the transformation to all employees. Mobile and digital technologies were dramatically altering the market, they told everybody, and if ING wanted to meet the expectations of customers, improve operations, and deploy new technological capabilities, it would have to become faster, leaner, and more flexible. To do that, they said, the company planned to make investments that would reduce costs and improve service. But it would also eliminate a significant number of jobs—at least a quarter of the total workforce.

Then came the *how*. Rather than letting the ax fall on select employees—a process that creates psychological trauma throughout a company—ING decided that almost everybody at the company, regardless of tenure or seniority, would be required to resign. After that, anybody who felt his or her attitude, capabilities, and skills would be a good fit at the "new" bank could apply to be rehired. That included Van den Boogert himself. Employees who did not get rehired would be supported by a program that would help them find jobs outside ING.

None of this made the company's transformation easy, of course. But according to Van den Boogert, the inclusive approach adopted by management significantly minimized the pain that employees felt during the transition, and it immediately set the new, smaller bank on the path to success. The employees who rejoined ING actively embraced its new mission, felt less survivor's remorse, and devoted themselves with excitement to the job of transformation. "When you talk about the *why, what,* and *how* at the same time," Van den Boogert told us, "people are going to challenge the *why* to prevent the *how*. But in this case, everyone had already been inspired by the *why* and *what*."

3. Look beyond the "spot market" for talent

Most successful companies have adopted increasingly aggressive strategies for finding critical high-skilled talent. Now they must expand that approach to include a wider range of employees. AT&T recognized that need in 2013, while developing its Workforce 2020 strategy, which focused on how the company would make the transition from a hardware-centric to a software-centric network.

The company had undergone a major transformation once before, in 1917, when it launched plans to use mechanical switchboards rather than human operators. But it carried that transformation out over the course of five decades! The Workforce 2020 transformation was much more complex and had to happen on a much faster timeline.

To get started, AT&T undertook a systematic audit of its quarter of a million employees to catalog their current skills and compare those with the skills it expected to need during and after its revamp. Ultimately, the company identified 100,000 employees whose jobs were likely to disappear, and several areas in which it would face skills and competency shortages. Armed with those insights, the company launched an ambitious, multiyear $1 billion initiative to develop an internal talent pipeline instead of simply playing the "spot market" for talent. In short, to meet its evolving needs, AT&T decided to make retraining available to its existing workforce. Since then, its employees have taken nearly 3 million online courses designed to help them acquire skills for new jobs in fields such as application development and cloud computing.

Already, this effort has yielded some unexpected benefits. The company now hires far fewer contractors to meet its needs for technical skills, for example. "We're shifting to employees," one of the company's top executives told CNBC this past March, "because we're starting to see the talent inside."

4. Collaborate to deepen the talent pool

In a fast-evolving environment, competing for talent doesn't work. It simply leads to a tragedy of the commons. Individual companies try to grab the biggest share of the skilled labor available, and these self-interested attempts just end up creating a shortage for all.

To avoid that problem, companies will have to fundamentally change their outlook and work together to ensure that the talent pool is constantly refreshed and updated. That will mean teaming up with other companies in the same industry or region to identify relevant skills, invest in developing curricula, and provide on-the-job training. It will also require forging new relationships for developing talent by, for instance, engaging with entrepreneurs and technology developers, partnering with educational institutions, and collaborating with policy makers.

U.S. utilities companies have already begun doing this. In 2006 they joined forces to establish the Center for Energy Workforce Development. The mission of the center, which has no physical office and is staffed primarily by former employees from member companies, is to figure out what jobs and skills the industry will need most as its older workers retire—and then how best to create a pipeline to meet those needs. "We're used to working together in this industry," Ann Randazzo, the center's executive director, told us. "When there's a storm, everybody gets in their trucks. Even if we compete in certain areas, including for workers, we've all got to work together to build this pipeline, or there just aren't going to be enough people."

The center quickly determined that three of the industry's most critical middle-skills jobs—linemen, field operators, and energy technicians—would be hit hard by the retirement of workers in the near future. Together, those three jobs make up almost 40% of a typical utility's workforce. To make sure they wouldn't go unfilled, CEWD implemented a two-pronged strategy. It created detailed tool kits, curricula, and training materials for all three jobs, which it made available free to utility companies; and it launched a grass-roots movement to reach out to next-generation workers and promote careers in the industry.

CEWD believes in connecting with promising talent early—very early. To that end, it has been working with hundreds of elementary, middle, and high schools to create materials and programs that introduce students to the benefits of working in the industry. These include a sense of larger purpose (delivering critical services to customers); stability (no offshoring of jobs, little technological displacement); the use of automation and technology to make jobs less physically taxing and more intellectually engaging; and, last but not least, surprisingly high wages. Describing the program to us, Randazzo said, "You're *growing* a workforce. We had to start from scratch to get students in the lower grades to understand what they need to do and to really be able to grow that all the way through high school to community colleges and universities. And it's not a one-and-done. We have to continually nurture it."

5. Find ways to manage chronic uncertainty

In today's world, managers know that if they don't swiftly identify and respond to shifts, their companies will be left behind. So how can firms best prepare?

The office-furniture manufacturer Steelcase has come up with some intriguing ideas. One is its Strategic Workforce Architecture and Transformation (SWAT) team, which tracks emerging trends and conducts real-time experiments in how to respond to them. The team has launched an internal platform called Loop, for example, where employees can volunteer to work on projects outside their own functions. This benefits both the company and its employees: As new needs arise, the company can quickly locate workers within its ranks who have the motivation and skills to meet them, and workers can gain experience and develop new capabilities in ways that their current jobs simply don't allow.

Employees at Steelcase have embraced Loop, and its success illustrates an idea that came through very clearly in our survey results. As Jill Dark, the director of the SWAT team, put it to us, "If you give people the opportunity to learn something new or to show their craft, they will give you their best work. The magic is in providing the opportunity."

That's a lesson that all managers should heed.

Originally published in May–June 2019. Reprint R1903H

How Apple Is Organized for Innovation

by Joel M. Podolny and Morten T. Hansen

APPLE IS WELL KNOWN FOR ITS innovations in hardware, software, and services. Thanks to them, it grew from some 8,000 employees and $7 billion in revenue in 1997, the year Steve Jobs returned, to 137,000 employees and $260 billion in revenue in 2019. Much less well known are the organizational design and the associated leadership model that have played a crucial role in the company's innovation success.

When Jobs arrived back at Apple, it had a conventional structure for a company of its size and scope. It was divided into business units, each with its own P&L responsibilities. General managers ran the Macintosh products group, the information appliances division, and the server products division, among others. As is often the case with decentralized business units, managers were inclined to fight with one another, over transfer prices in particular. Believing that conventional management had stifled innovation, Jobs, in his first year returning as CEO, laid off the general managers of all the business units (in a single day), put the entire company under one P&L, and combined the disparate functional departments of the business units into one functional organization. (See the exhibit "Apple's functional organization.")

Apple's functional organization

In 1997, when Steve Jobs returned to Apple, it had a conventional structure for its size and scope. It was divided into business units, each with its own P&L responsibilities. After retaking the helm, Jobs put the entire company under one P&L and combined the disparate departments of the business units into one functional organization that aligns expertise with decision rights—a structure Apple retains to this day.

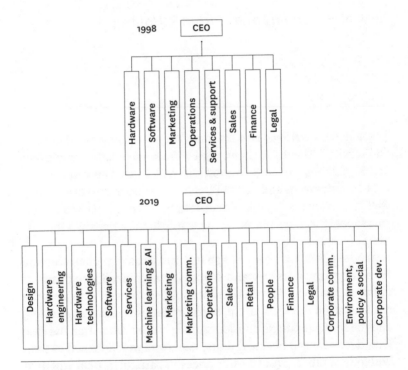

The adoption of a functional structure may have been unsurprising for a company of Apple's size at the time. What *is* surprising—in fact, remarkable—is that Apple retains it today, even though the company is nearly 40 times as large in terms of revenue and far more complex than it was in 1998. Senior vice presidents are in charge of functions, not products. As was the case with Jobs before him, CEO

Idea in Brief

The Challenge

Major companies competing in many industries struggle to stay abreast of rapidly changing technologies.

One Major Cause

They are typically organized into business units, each with its own set of functions. Thus the key deci-sion makers—the unit leaders—lack a deep understanding of all the domains that answer to them.

The Apple Model

The company is organized around functions, and expertise aligns with decision rights. Leaders are cross-functionally collaborative and deeply knowledgeable about details.

Tim Cook occupies the only position on the organizational chart where the design, engineering, operations, marketing, and retail of any of Apple's main products meet. In effect, besides the CEO, the company operates with no conventional general managers: people who control an entire process from product development through sales and are judged according to a P&L statement.

Business history and organizational theory make the case that as entrepreneurial firms grow large and complex, they must shift from a functional to a multidivisional structure to align accountability and control and prevent the congestion that occurs when countless decisions flow up the org chart to the very top. Giving business unit leaders full control over key functions allows them to do what is best to meet the needs of their individual units' customers and maximize their results, and it enables the executives overseeing them to assess their performance. As the Harvard Business School historian Alfred Chandler documented, U.S. companies such as DuPont and General Motors moved from a functional to a multidivisional structure in the early 20th century. By the latter half of the century the vast majority of large corporations had followed suit. Apple proves that this conventional approach is not necessary and that the functional structure may benefit companies facing tremendous technological change and industry upheaval.

Apple's commitment to a functional organization does not mean that its structure has remained static. As the importance of artificial intelligence and other new areas has increased, that structure has changed. Here we discuss the innovation benefits and leadership challenges of Apple's distinctive and ever-evolving organizational model, which may be useful for individuals and companies wanting to better understand how to succeed in rapidly changing environments.

Why a Functional Organization?

Apple's main purpose is to create products that enrich people's daily lives. That involves not only developing entirely new product categories such as the iPhone and the Apple Watch, but also continually innovating within those categories. Perhaps no product feature better reflects Apple's commitment to continuous innovation than the iPhone camera. When the iPhone was introduced, in 2007, Steve Jobs devoted only six seconds to its camera in the annual keynote event for unveiling new products. Since then iPhone camera technology has contributed to the photography industry with a stream of innovations: High dynamic range imaging (2010), panorama photos (2012), True Tone flash (2013), optical image stabilization (2015), the dual-lens camera (2016), portrait mode (2016), portrait lighting (2017), and night mode (2019) are but a few of the improvements.

To create such innovations, Apple relies on a structure that centers on functional expertise. Its fundamental belief is that those with the most expertise and experience in a domain should have decision rights for that domain. This is based on two views: First, Apple competes in markets where the rates of technological change and disruption are high, so it must rely on the judgment and intuition of people with deep knowledge of the technologies responsible for disruption. Long before it can get market feedback and solid market forecasts, the company must make bets about which technologies and designs are likely to succeed in smartphones, computers, and so on. Relying on technical experts rather than general managers increases the odds that those bets will pay off.

Second, Apple's commitment to offer the best possible products would be undercut if short-term profit and cost targets were the overriding criteria for judging investments and leaders. Significantly, the bonuses of senior R&D executives are based on company-wide performance numbers rather than the costs of or revenue from particular products. Thus product decisions are somewhat insulated from short-term financial pressures. The finance team is not involved in the product road map meetings of engineering teams, and engineering teams are not involved in pricing decisions.

We don't mean to suggest that Apple doesn't consider costs and revenue goals when deciding which technologies and features the company will pursue. It does, but in ways that differ from those employed by conventionally organized companies. Instead of using overall cost and price targets as fixed parameters within which to make design and engineering choices, R&D leaders are expected to weigh the benefits to users of those choices against cost considerations.

In a functional organization, individual and team reputations act as a control mechanism in placing bets. A case in point is the decision to introduce the dual-lens camera with portrait mode in the iPhone 7 Plus in 2016. It was a big wager that the camera's impact on users would be sufficiently great to justify its significant cost.

One executive told us that Paul Hubel, a senior leader who played a central role in the portrait mode effort, was "out over his skis," meaning that he and his team were taking a big risk: If users were unwilling to pay a premium for a phone with a more costly and better camera, the team would most likely have less credibility the next time it proposed an expensive upgrade or feature. The camera turned out to be a defining feature for the iPhone 7 Plus, and its success further enhanced the reputations of Hubel and his team.

It's easier to get the balance right between an attention to costs and the value added to the user experience when the leaders making decisions are those with deep expertise in their areas rather than general managers being held accountable primarily for meeting numerical targets. Whereas the fundamental principle of a conventional business unit structure is to align accountability and control, the fundamental principle of a functional organization is to align expertise and decision rights.

Thus the link between how Apple is organized and the type of innovations it produces is clear. As Chandler famously argued, "structure follows strategy"—even though Apple doesn't use the structure that he anticipated large multinationals would adopt. Now let's turn to the leadership model underlying Apple's structure.

Three Leadership Characteristics

Ever since Steve Jobs implemented the functional organization, Apple's managers at every level, from senior vice president on down, have been expected to possess three key leadership characteristics: deep expertise that allows them to meaningfully engage in all the work being done within their individual functions; immersion in the details of those functions; and a willingness to collaboratively debate other functions during collective decision-making. When managers have these attributes, decisions are made in a coordinated fashion by the people most qualified to make them.

Deep expertise

Apple is not a company where general managers oversee managers; rather, it is a company where experts lead experts. The assumption is that it's easier to train an expert to manage well than to train a manager to be an expert. At Apple, hardware experts manage hardware, software experts software, and so on. (Deviations from this principle are rare.) This approach cascades down all levels of the organization through areas of ever-increasing specialization. Apple's leaders believe that world-class talent wants to work for and with other world-class talent in a specialty. It's like joining a sports team where you get to learn from and play with the best.

Early on, Steve Jobs came to embrace the idea that managers at Apple should be experts in their area of management. In a 1984 interview he said, "We went through that stage in Apple where we went out and thought, *Oh, we're gonna be a big company, let's hire professional management.* We went out and hired a bunch of professional management. It didn't work at all. . . . They knew how to manage, but they didn't know how to *do* anything. If you're a great person, why do you want to work for somebody you can't learn anything from? And you know what's interesting? You know who the best managers are? They are the great individual contributors who never, ever want to be a manager but decide they have to be . . . because no one else is going to . . . do as good a job."

One current example is Roger Rosner, who heads Apple's software application business, which includes work-productivity apps such as Pages (word processing), Numbers (spreadsheets), and Keynote (presentations) along with GarageBand (music composition), iMovie (movie editing), and News (an app providing news content). Rosner, who studied electrical engineering at Carnegie Mellon, joined Apple in 2001 as a senior engineering manager and rose to become the director of iWork applications, the vice president of productivity apps, and since 2013 the VP of applications. With his deep expertise gained from previous experience as the director of engineering at several smaller software companies, Rosner exemplifies an expert leading experts.

In a functional organization, experts leading experts means that specialists create a deep bench in a given area, where they can learn from one another. For example, Apple's more than 600 experts on camera hardware technology work in a group led by Graham Townsend, a camera expert. Because iPhones, iPads, laptops, and desktop computers all include cameras, these experts would be scattered across product lines if Apple were organized in business units. That would dilute their collective expertise, reducing their power to solve problems and generate and refine innovations.

Immersion in the details

One principle that permeates Apple is "Leaders should know the details of their organization three levels down," because that is essential for speedy and effective cross-functional decision-making at the highest levels. If managers attend a decision-making meeting without the details at their disposal, the decision must either be made without the details or postponed. Managers tell war stories about making presentations to senior leaders who drill down into cells on a spreadsheet, lines of code, or a test result on a product.

Of course, the leaders of many companies insist that they and their teams are steeped in the details. But few organizations match Apple. Consider how its senior leaders pay extreme attention to the exact shape of products' rounded corners. The standard method for rounding corners is to use an arc of a circle to connect the perpendicular sides of a rectangular object, which produces a somewhat abrupt transition from straight to curve. In contrast, Apple's leaders insist on continuous curves, resulting in a shape known in the design community as a "squircle": The slope starts sooner but is less abrupt. (See the exhibit "One example of Apple's attention to detail.") An advantage of hardware products without abrupt changes in curvature is that they produce softer highlights (that is, little to no jump in light reflection along the corner). The difference is subtle, and executing on it isn't simply a matter of a more complicated mathematical formula. It demands that Apple's operations leaders commit to extremely precise manufacturing tolerances to produce millions of

---

One example of Apple's attention to detail

The standard method for rounding the corners of a rectangular object is to use an arc of a circle to connect the object's perpendicular sides. That can result in an abrupt transition in curvature. To produce softer highlights by minimizing light reflection, Apple uses a "squircle," which creates continuous curves.

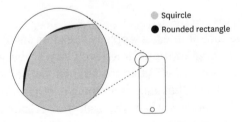

Squircle
Rounded rectangle

Source: Apple

---

iPhones and other products with squircles. This deep immersion in detail isn't just a concern that is pushed down to lower-level people; it is central at the leadership level.

Having leaders who are experts in their areas and can go deep into the details has profound implications for how Apple is run. Leaders can push, probe, and "smell" an issue. They know which details are important and where to focus their attention. Many people at Apple see it as liberating, even exhilarating, to work for experts, who provide better guidance and mentoring than a general manager would. Together, all can strive to do the best work of their lives in their chosen area.

Willingness to collaboratively debate

Apple has hundreds of specialist teams across the company, dozens of which may be needed for even one key component of a new product offering. For example, the dual-lens camera with portrait mode required the collaboration of no fewer than 40 specialist teams: silicon design, camera software, reliability engineering, motion sensor hardware, video engineering, core motion, and camera sensor design, to name just a few. How on earth does Apple develop and ship products that require such coordination? The answer is collaborative debate. Because no function is responsible for a product or a service on its own, cross-functional collaboration is crucial.

When debates reach an impasse, as some inevitably do, higher-level managers weigh in as tiebreakers, including at times the CEO and the senior VPs. To do this at speed with sufficient attention to detail is challenging for even the best of leaders, making it all the more important that the company fill many senior positions from within the ranks of its VPs, who have experience in Apple's way of operating.

However, given Apple's size and scope, even the executive team can resolve only a limited number of stalemates. The many horizontal dependencies mean that ineffective peer relationships at the VP and director levels have the potential to undermine not only particular projects but the entire company. Consequently, for people to attain and remain in a leadership position within a function, they must be highly effective collaborators.

That doesn't mean people can't express their points of view. Leaders are expected to hold strong, well-grounded views and advocate forcefully for them, yet also be willing to change their minds when presented with evidence that others' views are better. Doing so is not always easy, of course. A leader's ability to be both partisan and open-minded is facilitated by two things: deep understanding of and devotion to the company's values and common purpose, and a commitment to separating how *right* from how *hard* a particular path is so that the difficulty of executing a decision doesn't prevent its being selected.

The development of the iPhone's portrait mode illustrates a fanatical attention to detail at the leadership level, intense collaborative debate among teams, and the power of a shared purpose to shape and ultimately resolve debates. In 2009 Hubel had the idea of developing an iPhone feature that would allow people to take portrait photos with *bokeh*—a Japanese term that refers to the pleasing blurring of a background—which photography experts generally consider to be of the highest quality. At that time only expensive single-lens reflex cameras could take such photos, but Hubel thought that with a dual-lens design and advanced computational-photography techniques, Apple could add the capability in the iPhone. His idea aligned well with the camera team's stated purpose: "More people taking better images more of the time."

As the team worked to turn this idea into reality, several challenges emerged. The first attempts produced some amazing portrait pictures but also a number of "failure cases" in which the algorithm was unable to distinguish between the central object in sharp relief (a face, for instance) and the background being blurred. For example, if a person's face was to be photographed from behind chicken wire, it was not possible to construct an algorithm that would capture the chicken wire to the side of the face with the same sharpness as the chicken wire in front of it. The wire to the side would be as blurred as the background.

One might say, "Who cares about the chicken wire case? That's exceedingly rare." But for the team, sidestepping rare or extreme situations—what engineers call *corner cases*—would violate Apple's strict engineering standard of zero "artifacts," meaning "any undesired or unintended alteration in data introduced in a digital process by an involved technique and/or technology." Corner cases sparked "many tough discussions" between the camera team and other teams involved, recalls Myra Haggerty, the VP of sensor software and UX prototyping, who oversaw the firmware and algorithm teams. Sebastien Marineau-Mes, the VP to whom the camera software team ultimately reported, decided to defer the release of the feature until the following year to give the team time to better address failure cases—"a hard pill to swallow," Hubel admits.

To get some agreement on quality standards, the engineering teams invited senior design and marketing leaders to meet, figuring that they would offer a new perspective. The design leaders brought an additional artistic sensibility to the debate, asking, "What makes a beautiful portrait?" To help reassess the zero-artifacts standard, they collected images from great portrait photographers. They noted, among other things, that these photos often had blurring at the edges of a face but sharpness on the eyes. So they charged the algorithm teams with achieving the same effect. When the teams succeeded, they knew they had an acceptable standard.

Another issue that emerged was the ability to preview a portrait photo with a blurred background. The camera team had designed the feature so that users could see its effect on their photos only *after* they had been taken, but the human interface (HI) design team pushed back, insisting that users should be able to see a "live preview" and get some guidance about how to make adjustments *before* taking the photo. Johnnie Manzari, a member of the HI team, gave the camera team a demo. "When we saw the demo, we realized that this is what we needed to do," Townsend told us. The members of his camera hardware team weren't sure they could do it, but difficulty was not an acceptable excuse for failing to deliver what would clearly be a superior user experience. After months of engineering effort, a key stakeholder, the video engineering team (responsible for the low-level software that controls sensor and camera operations) found a way, and the collaboration paid off. Portrait mode was central to Apple's marketing of the iPhone 7 Plus. It proved a major reason for users' choosing to buy and delighting in the use of the phone.

As this example shows, Apple's collaborative debate involves people from various functions who disagree, push back, promote or reject ideas, and build on one another's ideas to come up with the best solutions. It requires open-mindedness from senior leaders. It also requires those leaders to inspire, prod, or influence colleagues in other areas to contribute toward achieving their goals.

While Townsend is accountable for how great the camera is, he needed dozens of other teams—each of which had a long list of its own commitments—to contribute their time and effort to the portrait mode project. At Apple that's known as *accountability without control:* You're accountable for making the project succeed even though you don't control all the other teams. This process can be messy yet produce great results. "Good mess" happens when various teams work with a shared purpose, as in the case of the portrait mode project. "Bad mess" occurs when teams push their own agendas ahead of common goals. Those who become associated with bad mess and don't or can't change their behavior are removed from leadership positions, if not from Apple altogether.

Leadership at Scale

Apple's way of organizing has led to tremendous innovation and success over the past two decades. Yet it has not been without challenges, especially with revenues and head count having exploded since 2008.

As the company has grown, entering new markets and moving into new technologies, its functional structure and leadership model have had to evolve. Deciding how to organize areas of expertise to best enable collaboration and rapid decision-making has been an important responsibility of the CEO. The adjustments Tim Cook has implemented in recent years include dividing the hardware function into hardware engineering and hardware technologies; adding artificial intelligence and machine learning as a functional area; and moving human interface out of software to merge it with industrial design, creating an integrated design function.

Another challenge posed by organizational growth is the pressure it imposes on the several hundred VPs and directors below the executive team. If Apple were to cap the size or scope of a senior leader's organization to limit the number and breadth of details that the leader is expected to own, the company would need to hugely expand the number of senior leaders, making the kind of collaboration that has worked so well impossible to preserve.

Cognizant of this problem, Apple has been quite disciplined about limiting the number of senior positions to minimize how many leaders must be involved in any cross-functional activity. In 2006, the year before the iPhone's launch, the company had some 17,000 employees; by 2019 that number had grown more than eightfold, to 137,000. Meanwhile, the number of VPs approximately doubled, from 50 to 96. The inevitable result is that senior leaders head larger and more diverse teams of experts, meaning more details to oversee and new areas of responsibility that fall outside their core expertise.

In response, many Apple managers over the past five years or so have been evolving the leadership approach described above: experts leading experts, immersion in the details, and collaborative debate. We have codified these adaptions in what we call the *discretionary leadership* model, which we have incorporated into a new educational program for Apple's VPs and directors. Its purpose is to address the challenge of getting this leadership approach to drive innovation in all areas of the company, not just product development, at an ever-greater scale.

When Apple was smaller, it may have been reasonable to expect leaders to be experts on and immersed in the details of pretty much everything going on in their organizations. However, they now need to exercise greater discretion regarding where and how they spend their time and efforts. They must decide which activities demand their full attention to detail because those activities create the most value for Apple. Some of those will fall within their existing core expertise (what they still need to *own*), and some will require them to *learn* new areas of expertise. Activities that require less attention from the leader can be pushed down to others (and the leaders will either *teach* others or *delegate* in cases where they aren't experts).

Rosner, the VP of applications, provides a good example. Like many other Apple managers, he has had to contend with three challenges arising from Apple's tremendous growth. First, the *size* of his function has exploded over the past decade in terms of both head count (from 150 to about 1,000) and the number of projects under way at any given time. Clearly, he cannot dive into all the details of all those projects. Second, the *scope* of his portfolio has widened: Over the past 10 years he has assumed responsibility for new applications, including News, Clips (video editing), Books, and Final Cut Pro (advanced video editing). Although apps are his core area of expertise, some aspects of these—among them editorial content for News, how book publishing works, and video editing—involve matters in which Rosner is not an expert. Finally, as Apple's product portfolio and number of projects have expanded, even more coordination with other functions is required, increasing the *complexity* of collaborating across the many units. For instance, whereas Rosner is responsible for the engineering side of News, other managers oversee the operating system on which it depends, the content, and the business relationships with content creators (such as the *New York Times*) and advertisers.

To cope, Rosner has adapted his role. As an expert who leads other experts, he had been immersed in details—especially those concerning the top-level aspects of software applications and their architecture that affect how users engage with the software. He also collaborated with managers across the company in projects that involved those areas.

But with the expansion of his responsibilities, he has moved some things from his *owning* box—including traditional productivity apps such as Keynote and Pages—into his *teaching* box. (See the exhibit "Roger Rosner's discretionary leadership.") Now he guides and gives feedback to other team members so that they can develop software applications according to Apple's norms. Being a teacher doesn't mean that Rosner gives instruction at a whiteboard; rather, he offers strong, often passionate critiques of his team's work. (Clearly, gen-

Roger Rosner's discretionary leadership

Apple's VP of applications, Roger Rosner, oversees a portfolio comprising four distinct categories that require varying amounts of his time and attention to detail. In 2019 it looked like this:

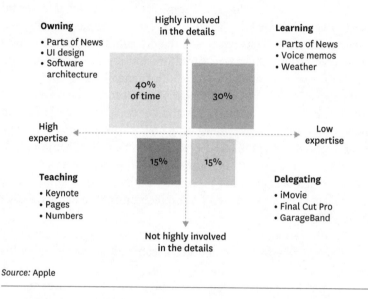

Owning
- Parts of News
- UI design
- Software architecture

Highly involved in the details

Learning
- Parts of News
- Voice memos
- Weather

40% of time

30%

High expertise

Low expertise

15%

15%

Teaching
- Keynote
- Pages
- Numbers

Delegating
- iMovie
- Final Cut Pro
- GarageBand

Not highly involved in the details

Source: Apple

eral managers without his core expertise would find it difficult to teach what they don't know.)

The second challenge for Rosner involved the addition of activities beyond his original expertise. Six years ago he was given responsibility for the engineering and design of News. Consequently, he had to learn about publishing news content via an app—to understand news publications, digital advertising, machine learning to personalize news content, architecting for privacy, and how to incentivize publishers. Thus some of his work fell into the *learning* box. Here managers face a steep learning curve to acquire new skills. Given how demanding this is, only critical new activities should fall into this category. Over six years of intense learning, Rosner has mastered some of these areas, which are now in his owning box.

As long as a particular activity remains in the learning box, leaders must adopt a beginner's mindset, questioning subordinates in a way that suggests they don't already know the answer (because they don't). This differs starkly from the way leaders question subordinates about activities in the owning and teaching boxes.

Finally, Rosner has delegated some areas—including iMovie and GarageBand, in which he is not an expert—to people with the requisite capabilities. For activities in the *delegating* box, he assembles teams, agrees on objectives, monitors and reviews progress, and holds the teams accountable: the stuff of general management.

Whereas Apple's VPs spend most of their time in the owning and learning boxes, general managers at other companies tend to spend most of their time in the delegating box. Rosner estimates that he spends about 40% of his time on activities he owns (including collaboration with others in a given area), about 30% on learning, about 15% on teaching, and about 15% on delegating. These numbers vary by manager, of course, depending on their business and the needs at a given time.

The discretionary leadership model preserves the fundamental principle of an effective functional organization at scale—aligning expertise and decision rights. Apple can effectively move into new areas when leaders like Rosner take on new responsibilities outside their original expertise, and teams can grow in size when leaders teach others their craft and delegate work. We believe that Apple will continue to innovate and prosper by being organized this way.

Apple's functional organization is rare, if not unique, among very large companies. It flies in the face of prevailing management theory that companies should be reorganized into divisions and business units as they become large. But something vital gets lost in a shift to business units: the alignment of decision rights with expertise.

Why do companies so often cling to having general managers in charge of business units? One reason, we believe, is that making the change is difficult. It entails overcoming inertia, reallocating power among managers, changing an individual-oriented incentive system, and learning new ways of collaborating. That is daunting when a company already faces huge external challenges. An intermediate step may be to cultivate the experts-leading-experts model even within a business unit structure. For example, when filling the next senior management role, pick someone with deep expertise in that area as opposed to someone who might make the best general manager. But a full-fledged transformation requires that leaders also transition to a functional organization. Apple's track record proves that the rewards may justify the risks. Its approach can produce extraordinary results.

Originally published in November–December 2020. Reprint R2006F

Digital Transformation Comes Down to Talent in Four Key Areas

by Thomas H. Davenport and Thomas C. Redman

OVER THE YEARS, WE'VE PARTICIPATED in, advised on, or studied hundreds of digital transformations. In doing so, we've gained a perspective on just how difficult true digital transformation really is and what it takes to succeed. Digital transformation is not for the faint of heart—the unfortunate reality is that, to date, many such efforts, like transformation programs in general, have failed.

Success requires bringing together and coordinating a far greater range of effort than most leaders appreciate. A poor showing in any one of four interrelated domains—technology, data, process, or organizational change capability—can scuttle an otherwise well-conceived transformation. The really important stuff, from creating and communicating a compelling vision, to crafting a plan and adjusting it on the fly, to slogging through the details, is all about people.

More than anything else, digital transformation requires talent. Indeed, assembling the right team of technology, data, and process people who can work together—with a strong leader who can bring about change—may be the single most important step that a company contemplating digital transformation can take. Of course, even the best talent does not assure success. But a lack of it almost guarantees failure.

Let's explore the talent needed in each of the four domains in turn.

Technology

From the Internet of Things to blockchain to data lakes to artificial intelligence, the raw potential of emerging technologies is staggering. And while many of these are becoming easier to use, understanding how any particular technology contributes to transformational opportunity, adapting that technology to the specific needs of the business, and integrating it with existing systems are all extremely complex. Complicating matters, most companies have enormous technical debt—embedded legacy technologies that are difficult to change. You can only resolve these issues with people who have technological depth and breadth—and the ability to work hand in hand with the business.

Challenging as these difficulties are, an even more critical issue is that many businesspeople have lost faith in their IT department's ability to drive major change, as many IT functions are primarily focused on "keeping the lights on." Eventually, however, digital transformation must incorporate institutional IT, so rebuilding trust is essential. This means that technologists must provide, and demonstrate, business value with every technology innovation. Thus, leaders of the technology domain must be great communicators, and they must have the strategic sense to make technological choices that balance innovation with mitigating technical debt.

Data

The unfortunate reality is that at many companies today most data is not up to basic standards, and the rigors of transformation require much better data quality and analytics. Transformation almost cer-

Idea in Brief

Digital transformation requires talent. Assembling the right team of people in four domains—technology, data, process, and organizational change capacity—may be the single most important step that a company contemplating digital transformation can take. Each of these areas requires a certain set of skills.

In the technology domain, you need people with technological depth and breadth, and the ability to work hand-in-hand with the business. Leaders of the technology domain must be great communicators, and they must have strategic sense. You'll need this same breadth and depth in the next domain: data. You also need the ability to convince large numbers of people at the front lines of organizations to take on new roles as data customers and data creators.

When considering the next domain, process, look for the ability to "herd cats"—to align silos and to know when incremental process improvement is sufficient or when radical process reengineering is necessary. Finally, for organizational change capability, look for leadership, teamwork, courage, emotional intelligence, and other elements of change management.

tainly involves understanding new types of unstructured data (e.g., a driver-supplied picture of damage to a car), sourcing and making sense of massive quantities of data external to your company, leveraging proprietary data, and integrating everything together, all while shedding enormous quantities of data that have never been (and never will be) used. Data presents an interesting paradox: Most companies know data is important and they know quality is bad, yet they waste enormous resources by failing to put the proper roles and responsibilities in place. They often blame their IT functions for all these failures.

As with technology, you need talent with both great breadth and depth in data. Even more important is the ability to convince large numbers of people at the front lines of organizations to take on new roles as data customers and data creators. This means thinking through and communicating the data they need now and the data they'll need after transformation. It also means helping frontline workers to improve their own work processes and tasks so that they create data correctly.

Process

Transformation requires an end-to-end mindset, a rethinking of ways to meet customer needs, seamless connection of work activities, and the ability to manage across silos going forward. A process orientation is a natural fit with these needs. But many have found process management—horizontally, across silos, and focused on customers—difficult to reconcile with traditional hierarchical thinking. As a result, this powerful concept has languished. Without it, transformation is reduced to a series of incremental improvements—important and helpful but not truly transformative.

In building talent in this domain, look for the ability to "herd cats"—aligning silos in the direction of the customer to improve existing processes and design new ones—and a strategic sense to know when incremental process improvement is sufficient and when radical process reengineering is necessary.

Organizational Change Capability

In this domain we include leadership, teamwork, courage, emotional intelligence, and other elements of change management. Fortunately, much has been written about this domain for many years, so we won't review it here, other than to note that anyone responsible for digital transformation must be well-versed in the area. While we have no firm evidence to support this, it seems that those who gravitate toward technology, data, and process are somewhat less likely to embrace the human side of change. Of course, in our recommendations above, we have urged leaders to seek those with excellent people skills. If you are unable to find them, a good alternative is to put some "purple people," those able to work on both sides, on the transformation team.

Pulling It All Together

So far, we've discussed the technology, data, process, and organizational change capability domains as if they existed in isolation, which, of course, they don't. Rather, they are part of a larger whole. Technology is the engine of digital transformation, data is the fuel, process is the guidance system, and organizational change capability is the landing gear. You need them all, and they must function well together.

Consider the "our systems don't talk" problem, which bedevils most companies and is anathema to digital transformation. But in which domain does it belong? On first glance, it appears to be a tech problem—but it also leads to enormous process inefficiencies. Yet it stems from a lack of solid data architecture, and it may involve organizational structure and politics issues that are difficult to change. So one could argue that any domain should take the lead. But the best solution involves the four working together.

Absent a deep understanding of each domain, it is difficult for nearly all business leaders to see the full potential in digital transformation—a contributing factor to many failed digital transformations. But of course, no one individual possesses all the required knowledge and capability. Hence our call to assemble talent in each area.

Finally, work on technology, data, and process must proceed in an appropriate sequence. It is generally accepted that there is no sense automating a process that doesn't work, so in many cases, process improvement or reengineering must come first. On the other hand, some transformations will feature large doses of artificial intelligence. Since bad data stymies development and deployment of good AI models, in these cases, work on data should come first. Start with your end goals, then develop the sequence of steps best suited to achieving them.

Digital transformation can and should be focused on problems of greatest need to the company. Those priorities will also lend a flavor to the talent needed; if the focus is on transforming customer relationships, for example, the data talent on the team may have particular expertise in customer data, the process talent on sales and marketing processes, and so forth. More important, however, is that the talent possesses the four types of expertise we have described and has had previous success at creating and executing on any kind of technology-driven transformation.

Originally published on hbr.org on May 21, 2020. Reprint H05N4Y

LEANDRO DALLEMULE is the chief data officer at AIG.

THOMAS H. DAVENPORT is the President's Distinguished Professor in Management and Information Technology at Babson College, a research fellow at the MIT Initiative on the Digital Economy, and a senior adviser at Deloitte Analytics. He is the author of over a dozen management books, most recently *Only Humans Need Apply: Winners and Losers in the Age of Smart Machines* and *The AI Advantage*.

ALICE DE CHALENDAR is a consultant at BCG and a researcher at the BCG Henderson Institute.

TIM FOUNTAINE is a partner in McKinsey's Sydney office and leads QuantumBlack, an advanced analytics firm owned by McKinsey, in Australia.

JOSEPH B. FULLER is a professor of management practice and a co-chair of the Project on Managing the Future of Work at Harvard Business School. He is also the faculty cochair of the HBS executive education program Leading an Agile Workforce Transformation.

NATHAN FURR is a strategy professor at INSEAD and a coauthor of *Innovation Capital* (Harvard Business Review Press, 2019), *Leading Transformation* (Harvard Business Review Press, 2018), and *The Innovator's Method* (Harvard Business Review Press, 2014).

MORTEN T. HANSEN is a professor at the University of California, Berkeley, and a faculty member at Apple University. He is the author of *Great at Work and Collaboration* and coauthor of *Great by Choice*. He has been named one of the top management thinkers in the world by Thinkers50. Find him on Twitter: @MortentHansen.

JAMES E. HEPPELMANN is the president and CEO of PTC, a leading maker of industrial software.

MARCO IANSITI is the David Sarnoff Professor of Business Administration at Harvard Business School, where he heads the Technology and Operations Management Unit and the Digital Initiative. He has advised many companies in the technology sector, including Microsoft, Facebook, and Amazon. He is a coauthor of the book *Competing in the Age of AI* (Harvard Business Review Press, 2020).

STELIOS KAVADIAS is the Margaret Thatcher Professor of Enterprise Studies in Innovation and Growth at the University of Cambridge's Judge Business School and the director of its Entrepreneurship Centre.

KOSTAS LADAS is an associate at the Entrepreneurship Centre at Cambridge's Judge Business School.

KARIM R. LAKHANI is the Charles Edward Wilson Professor of Business Administration and the Dorothy and Michael Hintze Fellow at Harvard Business School and the founder and codirector of the Laboratory for Innovation Science at Harvard. He is a coauthor of the book *Competing in the Age of AI* (Harvard Business Review Press, 2020).

AARON LEVIE is a cofounder and the CEO of Box, one of the world's fastest-growing cloud software vendors.

CHRISTOPH LOCH is a professor at and the director of the University of Cambridge's Judge Business School.

BRIAN MCCARTHY is a partner in McKinsey's Atlanta office and co-leads the knowledge development agenda for McKinsey Analytics.

RITA MCGRATH is a professor at Columbia Business School and a globally recognized expert on strategy in uncertain and volatile environments. She is the author of *The End of Competitive Advantage* (Harvard Business Review Press, 2013) and, most recently, *Seeing Around Corners.*

RYAN MCMANUS is the CEO of Techtonic.io and a globally recognized expert on digital business models, transformation, and ecosystems. He is on multiple public and private boards and is a contributing lecturer at Columbia Business School.

JOEL M. PODOLNY is the dean and vice president of Apple University in Cupertino, California. The former dean of the Yale School of Management, Podolny was also a professor at Harvard Business School and the Stanford Graduate School of Business.

MICHAEL E. PORTER is a University Professor at Harvard, based at Harvard Business School. He is a coauthor of *The Politics Industry: How Political Innovation Can Break Partisan Gridlock and Save Our Democracy* (Harvard Business Review Press, 2020).

MANJARI RAMAN is a program director and senior researcher for Harvard Business School's Project on U.S. Competitiveness and the Project on Managing the Future of Work.

THOMAS C. REDMAN, "the Data Doc," is the president of Data Quality Solutions. He helps companies and people, including startups, multinationals, executives, and leaders at all levels, chart their courses to data-driven futures. He places special emphasis on quality, analytics, and organizational capabilities.

TAMIM SALEH is a senior partner in McKinsey's London office and heads McKinsey Analytics in Europe.

ANDREW SHIPILOV is the John H. Loudon Chaired Professor of International Management at INSEAD. He is a coauthor of *Network Advantage: How to Unlock Value From Your Alliances and Partnerships*.

ROBERT SIEGEL is a lecturer in management at the Stanford University Graduate School of Business. He is also a partner at XSeed Capital.

NICOLAJ SIGGELKOW is a professor of management and strategy at Wharton and a codirector of the Mack Institute for Innovation Management. He is a coauthor of *Connected Strategy* (Harvard Business Review Press, 2019).

CHRISTIAN TERWIESCH is a professor of operations and innovation at Wharton and a codirector of the Mack Institute for Innovation Management. He is a coauthor of *Connected Strategy* (Harvard Business Review Press, 2019).

JUDITH K. WALLENSTEIN is a senior partner and managing director at Boston Consulting Group, a BCG Fellow, and the director of the BCG Henderson Institute in Europe.

MAXWELL WESSEL is the general manager of SAP.iO, a lecturer at Stanford's Graduate School of Business, and an investor with Nextgen Venture Partners. Connect with him on Twitter @maxwellelliot.

Index